Writing *on the* Bus

This book is part of the Peter Lang Education list.
Every volume is peer reviewed and meets
the highest quality standards for content and production.

PETER LANG
New York • Washington, D.C./Baltimore • Bern
Frankfurt • Berlin • Brussels • Vienna • Oxford

RICHARD KENT

Writing *on the* Bus

Using Athletic Team Notebooks and Journals to Advance Learning and Performance in Sports

PETER LANG
New York • Washington, D.C./Baltimore • Bern
Frankfurt • Berlin • Brussels • Vienna • Oxford

Library of Congress Cataloging-in-Publication Data

Kent, Richard.
Writing on the bus: using athletic team notebooks and journals
to advance learning and performance in sports / Richard Kent.
p. cm.
Includes bibliographical references and index.
1. Athletes—Training of. 2. Coaching (Athletics)
3. English language—Composition and exercises. I. Title.
GV711.5.K48 613.711—dc23 2011030854
ISBN 978-1-4331-1684-1 (hardcover)
ISBN 978-1-4331-1651-3 (paperback)
ISBN: 978-1-4539-0187-8 (e-book)

Bibliographic information published by **Die Deutsche Nationalbibliothek**.
Die Deutsche Nationalbibliothek lists this publication in the "Deutsche Nationalbibliografie"; detailed bibliographic data is available on the Internet at http://dnb.d-nb.de/.

This book is published in cooperation with the National Writing Project, University of California, 2105 Bancroft Way, Berkeley, CA 94720.

The paper in this book meets the guidelines for permanence and durability of the Committee on Production Guidelines for Book Longevity of the Council of Library Resources.

Printed in the United States of America

For Brenda and Joe Sassi

Team notebooks create a different way for players to learn.

—Mike Keller, Head Coach
University of Southern Maine Men's Soccer

Our team had never been so in tune with themselves . . . with team notebooks the players took ownership of their team and destiny. We had the most successful season in program history.

—Amy Edwards, Head Coach
Gonzaga University Women's Soccer
—former Associate Head Coach, University of Missouri

I like free writing . . . it's a meditation, trying to open up the mind and go for it.

—David Chamberlain
Nor/Am SuperTour Cross-Country Ski Champion
US Nordic World Championship Team

Writing provides another avenue for strengthening the player/coach relationship.

—Brian Bold, Head Coach
Burnt Hills-Ballston Lake Soccer

No one likes skiing with a cluttered mind, so put it on paper and free some space.

—Carter Robertson, Alpine Ski Racer
Burke Mountain Academy

Contents

Foreword xi
Acknowledgments xv

Introduction 1
1. A Glimpse at Athletic Team Notebooks 7
2. Preseason Thoughts: Looking Back, Thinking Forward, and Making Plans 29
3. Competition Analysis I: Telling the Story of Your Game 55
4. Competition Analysis II: Telling the Story of Their Game 73
5. Postseason Thoughts: Looking Back, Thinking Forward, and Making Plans . . . Again 85
6. Notes, Worksheets, and Activities 95
7. Athletes' Journals 105
8. Athlete's Journal: Creating a Template 129
9. David's Story: Writing toward the Podium 147
10. FAQs 165

Conclusion 183

References 187
Index 191

Foreword

A story about sports and language.

In my sophomore year in high school I was a member of the cross-country team. I joined mainly to get ready for track season, but I came to love the early fall practices on the town's golf course—and looked forward to the first meet on the grounds of Worthington High School, north of Columbus. As I recall, the course began in a big open lawn in front of the school and went toward the expansive athletic fields. After about a quarter mile the course plunged down a steep hill onto a long flat stretch.

As the gun went off I felt myself propelled by the mass of runners, almost sprinting across that open area—by the time I reached the hill I was beginning to breathe heavily and the charge down the hill felt completely uncontrolled, my arms windmilling. Within minutes I was gasping for breath, panicked; I slowed down, runners passed me in waves. I tried to regain my breath but couldn't keep from gasping for air. I slowed to a walk. I dropped to one knee—a race official then came over to me to ask me how I was doing and to walk me off the course.

I still vividly recall the feeling of defeat, embarrassment, and shame that overwhelmed me at that moment. I had *quit*. I was therefore a *quitter*. It was the only story I could tell myself about that race, the only explanation I could come up with ("A winner never quits and a quitter never wins."). I truly believed that my problem was a deep flaw in character or willpower—I wasn't cut out for this sport (though I ran well in practice). I could feel my coach's disapproval and disappointment when I told him. We didn't talk about it, and I'm not sure I would have known how to explain it, or he would have known how to help.

In retrospect, and with the help of this wonderful book, I could imagine a different outcome. If my coach and I had thought about it together, or I had written about it then (and not just now, 45 years later), I might have come to a different and less self-condemning conclusion. We might have gotten past the shame of the moment to realize that I had simply made a serious mistake in pacing (and probably a failure to warm up properly). It was, after all, my first race and my first time away from the familiarity of my home course. My difficulty was not the result of a lack of willpower or flawed character, but the physiological effect of these mistakes—ones that could be corrected in future races.

We might have developed a strategy to determine the best early pace for me, one that would allow me to even accelerate in the latter parts of the race. As I began to feel comfortable in that early pace, I could gradually have made it faster, and moved toward a more even pace in subsequent races. In other words, I could have learned to take control and avoid that desperate feeling of complete breathlessness.

But we needed a language to do this reflection; we needed something more than the rough, macho code of winners and losers. As it turned out, those 8 or 9 minutes on the Worthington course haunted my experience in cross-country.

This book provides those analytic invitations that would have been so useful to me. It is full of practical ideas for using a variety of journals (individual and team), questionnaires, writing prompts, self-profiles, and letters. But underlying this great practicality is, I believe, a distinctive vision of the athlete—and the coach. Competitive sport, as Rich Kent perceives it, involves intense and continuous reflection, what John Dewey called "intelligence." By that, Dewey meant the ability to locate and name problems, to devise plans, to test them in practice—then to revise plans and begin the cycle again.

This cycle of reflection helps keep the athlete on a more even keel and in a productive emotional range. There is little place for grandiosity and gloating, or for the pure self-condemnation that I felt after my race. One thing that always stuns me about top-class athletes is their ability to work in this emotional range. I marvel at their ability to absorb failure (often very public failure) and to turn it into a *technical* problem; they name it, learn from it, plan changes, then put it in the past, and move forward. Coaches, good ones at least, contribute to this process. I suspect that athletes who can't find this range, whatever their "natural" abilities, don't last long at the top levels.

If this book did nothing else other than lay out these opportunities for reflective writing, it would be a useful guide for coaches. But the book is more than a set of suggested practices; it is filled with examples of Rich Kent and other coaches interacting with their athletes. We get excerpts from the writing of coaches at all levels, and from athletes—high school soccer players to world class skiers. And particularly through his own example, Kent teaches us how to read this writing—generously, thoughtfully, learning from the experiences of his athletes, even appreciating their goofy humor. He has the ability to pull nuggets of insight from writing that a less alert and sympathetic reader would miss. He is the kind of teacher who makes you feel smart.

This is a quality of Kent's teaching that I have admired since I came to know him at Mountain Valley High School. He has the gift of truly great teachers—of seeing a better version of students (and athletes) than they themselves see. This book conveys his deep affection for athletics and athletes, his belief that it is a great privilege to be allowed entry into their lives and thinking.

And how better to enter into this world than through writing?

Thomas Newkirk
Durham, NH

Acknowledgments

Perhaps the first draft of this book began on a flight back from England in the early 1980s. After 2 weeks of games, practices, and touring, I asked my players to write about our soccer trip, and they did. When I read their words, something clicked. To those athletes, and many more through the years, thank you for sharing your words and wisdom.

When I asked U.S. Skier David Chamberlain if I could interview him about his journal writing, he said yes. Then, characteristic of this masterful skier and person, David opened the door to his racing, writing, and life for the next 5 years. I owe him a great debt.

For the past 6 years, many coaches and athletes have shared their stories and ideas in email, via Skype, over the phone, and in person; some of these generous individuals are named in the book—many are not. All of you have my thanks for your willingness to share.

In the long haul of this book, Amy Edwards of Gonzaga University offered insightful commentary for the better part of 3 years about her team's use of Team Notebooks. Mike Keller of the University of Southern Maine allowed me to conduct a season-long study of his team's use of Team Notebooks in 2006.

I am indebted to the coaches, athletes, and staff of the Burke Mountain Academy in East Burke, Vermont. Special thanks to Tom DeCarlo, Burke's Academic Director, for welcoming me to this little mountainside school that can and does.

Much of the theory and practice behind Athletic Team Notebooks and Journals may be attributed to my work and learning as a member of the National Writing Project. And at the University of Maine, my Maine Writing Project friends have been spirited and important colleagues.

For her organizational skills and athletic insights a big thank-you to Kaili Jordan Phillips, my UMaine research assistant—now a brilliant English teacher.

The staff at Peter Lang Publishing is expedient and careful . . . this is particularly true of Sophie Appel, Design and Production Supervisor. I especially value Chris Myers, managing director, for his chutzpah and faith in taking on this project.

Throughout the day-to-day writing of this book, my friend Gayle Sirois worked skillfully as reader, editor, and advocate.

No writer could have a more gifted editor than Anne Wood. For over 30 years, Anne has found just the right words to help me find my own. She is the dearest of friends.

Introduction

A dozen years into this new century and just about every athlete I know is writing.

Some keep blogs and others maintain Facebook sites—it's mind-boggling how many Twitter. Professional athletes work with sport psychologists, fine-tuning their mental approaches to training and games through talk, imagery, meditation, and writing. If you played basketball at Duke University for Coach Gail Goestenkors, 2006 U.S. Basketball National Coach of the Year, you kept a journal. If you played college soccer for Mike Keller at the University of Southern Maine or Amy Edwards at Gonzaga University, you kept a Team Notebook. Olympians and world-class athletes in all sports keep training logs and exchange reflective email with advisors, coaches, and training partners.

As you'll read later in the book, tennis champion Serena Williams pulled out her journal book for the press at Wimbledon in 2007, and for those baseball fans who followed the phenomenal Red Sox teams of the mid-2000s, they witnessed all-star pitcher Curt Schilling on the bench between innings . . . writing.

In England, 16-year-old soccer players who become apprentices to professional teams are *required* to keep a journal about training sessions, games, diet. . . . And if your goal is to make the U.S. Ski Team and are fortunate enough to land a spot at the renowned Burke Mountain Academy in Vermont . . . there's a good chance that writing will be a part of your training. What's this all about, you ask? It's about learning.

Ways Coaches Learn

In 1984, soccer was relatively new to Maine public schools. The season lasted 10 short weeks and most teams played their matches on American football fields—a space too small for *the beautiful game.* To build the capacity of the state's program for players and coaches alike, we organized trips to England, the motherland of our sport.

Rain plagued our 1984 England tour. At the first game on the outskirts of London, the pitch was a quagmire. Most of my players wore soccer shoes with short, stubby cleats—*molded soles,* we called them—while the British schoolboys screwed in foul-weather studs about three-quarters of an inch long. The Maine boys played athletically and with dogged determination—but inevitably, with those shoes, the British kids stood up and scored . . . and we did not. My players learned and so did their coach. For the next tour, I revised the players' equipment list.

While conducting a series of studies with various athletic teams, the genesis of this book, I asked coaches how they honed their skills. The answers were not surprising. We learn by reading books and articles, attending clinics, and watching videos. We email colleagues and talk on the phone. We learn from the John Woodens and the Pat Summits of the world and also by discussing our sports with athletes, officials, and fans. When interviewed by sports reporters, we are pushed to unpack, rethink, and diagnose our games.

Some of us learn by giving clinics to coaching colleagues; others continue to play our sport, officiate, and write articles. A few of us went to college to study coaching and most of us have been certified as coaches by our sports associations or through organizations like The National

Federation of State High School Associations. All of us learn by coaching games and thinking about our decisions, especially after a loss.

Ultimately, our work as coaches is about teaching and learning. Using a variety of instructional activities, we help our players move toward mastery. From analyzing game films to critiquing drills at the blocking sled, we devise multiple ways to teach our players. Those who study learning and teaching would agree: The meaning of our work as coaches is in the games we prepare our athletes to play. And those games, many of us know, provide quintessential life lessons.

Throughout our careers, we gather strands of knowledge and weave that learning into our coaching systems. We do this work to fortify our sports classrooms—the pools, fields, tracks, courses, rinks, half pipes, jumps, courts, and arenas where we guide our students toward outgrowing themselves. Our vocation centers on learning and teaching. Our goal: that elusive next level of play . . . and a winning record.

Ways Athletes Learn

Our athletes learn in a variety of ways, too. Some are skillful listeners and have the ability to translate our half-time talks into ESPN highlights. Other players don't hear a *single word we say* and return to the game as if they'd spent the halftime visiting their grandmothers and eating peanut butter fudge. For those athletes, we adapt our approach by sketching plays, writing lists, or asking questions one-on-one. Sometimes, we bench the kid—it just depends.

At the elite level of distance sports, athletes learn by monitoring their lactate levels and then fine-tuning their training. Within the high school ranks, coaches may require their athletes to referee or coach youth sports to develop a unique lens on the game, a view beyond the player's. To be sure, there are as many ways to learn as there are athletes as illustrated in Figure 1.

Although just about every athlete that I know writes, few athletic teams have an organized approach to include writing. When that's the case, an effective learning tool is neglected. In terms of communication, player development, and learning, writing has the potential to offer a powerful difference in the world of athletics.

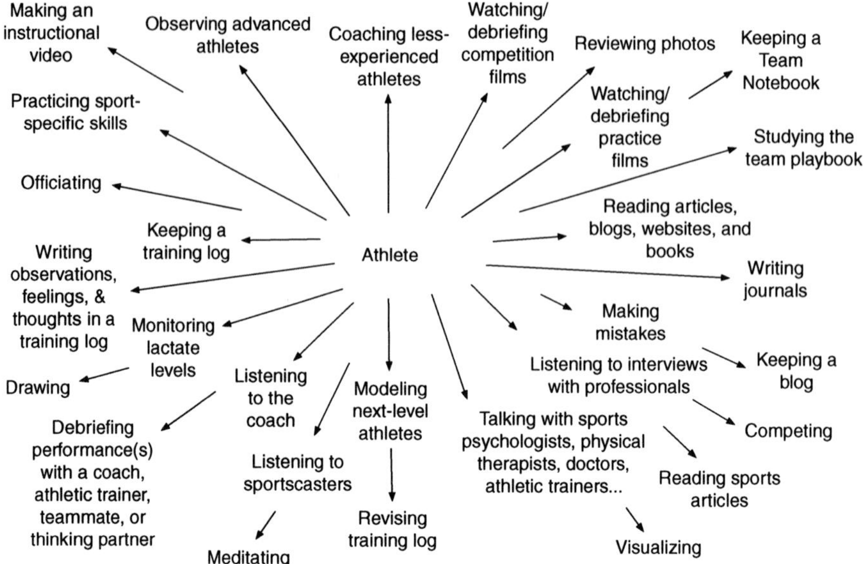

Figure 1 Some of the Ways Athletes Learn

Why Writing?

> "Writing organizes and clarifies our thoughts. Writing is how we think our way into a subject and make it our own. Writing enables us to find out what we know—and what we don't know—about whatever we're trying to learn."
>
> –*Writing to Learn* by William Zinsser (1989, Harper & Row)

It's not as if coaches don't have enough to do. However, the plain fact is that having athletes take a few minutes to write in an Athletic Team Notebook or Journal enhances communication and amplifies learning. As learning tools, notebooks and journals serve as a place for athletes to analyze and reflect. They engage seniors and first-year students, all-stars and benchwarmers—in different ways. And that difference is the beauty of such a learning activity.

For coaches, reading an athlete's writing adds a new dimension to our sports classrooms and to the learning that can make us more effective teachers of that sport. Indeed, effective coaching is the constant search for ways to enhance our athletes' learning so that they may move to the next level of play. As a result of reading Team Notebooks, we come to know our athletes and teams through a new lens: the written word. This additional way of knowing can help us further understand our athletes' strengths and challenges, and thereby assist us in creating more valuable training plans and practice sessions.

Of course, adding Team Notebooks to a program won't make up for unfit athletes, ill-designed training sessions, or tactical mistakes. But writing will complement an athletic program and add a new level of understanding for athletes and team staff members. The act of writing not only organizes and clarifies an athlete's thoughts, but for a team writing can also

- add variety to practice sessions,
- frontload pre- and post-game discussions,
- keep coaches and other team personnel informed in another way, and
- fill in knowledge gaps.

Ultimately, writing improves learning and that makes for more effective coaches, athletes, and teams.

But will writing help us win?

My Experiences as a Coach and Emerging Researcher

The mere mention of the word research used to make my brain seize up. As an apprentice coach in the classroom of David "Dusty" Drew at the University of Maine at Portland-Gorham (now the University of Southern Maine), I turned glassy-eyed when Coach Drew or any of my instructors made comments like "the research has shown us that . . . ." But once I stepped onto the playing fields and ski slopes as "the coach," my attitude changed as I faced scores of athletes who wanted, expected, and in some rare cases demanded that I guide them to that elusive next level.

My athletes' demands and the inevitable evolution of my sports of skiing and soccer ushered me to employ methods associated with action research, a kind of research in which "participants examine their own educational practice systematically and carefully" (Ferrance, 2000). An example occurred in the mid-1980s when the cross-country ski-racing world abruptly abandoned its classic skiing technique and turned to a faster method called skating or freestyle. At first, I tried to learn the technique by watching and evaluating World Cup ski racers on videos, talking with coaching colleagues, experimenting on my own skis, and teaching my own ski athletes the technique through trial and error. Very soon, I knew I needed more.

That more meant trucking 6 and a half hours west to Lake Placid's Mt. Van Hoevenberg Cross-Country Skiing Center, the site of the 1980 Winter Olympics, to learn this new ski technique and accompanying training activities. Within hours of arriving in Lake Placid, I was sucking wind on the notorious Russian Hill trying to keep up with my instructor, Muffy Ritz. A former U.S. Ski Team member, Muffy carried an oversized backpack full of equipment (remember those early-generation VHS cameras?) while the rest of us donned our 24-oz water bottles in fanny packs and struggled to keep Muffy in sight.

Attending a coaching clinic does provide an arena for research—the kind of inquiry where one turns to experts and the work they have produced (e.g., another coach's training plans). And yes, knowing what I know now I probably should have listened more closely to Coach Drew in college. The thing is, athletic coaches are involved in elements of action research on a daily basis: we identify a problem on our teams or with an athlete; we gather data or ideas about the problem; we review the data and ideas, and at times seek out feedback from colleagues and athletes; we revise our practices accordingly and employ new or modified approaches; and finally, we evaluate the results and either adapt those results or move forward with the new method. I would argue that the way we think about this cycle, and our purposefulness, contributes to our effectiveness as coaches. And, I'd contend, writing can play a role.

And so . . .

Through the years I have examined the writing of student, professional, and master athletes. These sources, plus the works of learning and composition theorists, have informed my thinking about writing as a way to learn in athletics. Perhaps most of all, however, the words written by my own athletes have led me to understand the promise of Athletic Team Notebooks and Journals.

Chapter One

A Glimpse at Athletic Team Notebooks

One of the first times I asked an entire team to write, we were on a flight back from England. I asked the 16- and 17-year-olds on the select team to write because I wanted a clearer sense of their views of the 2-week experience, including our games, the practice sessions, the professional matches we attended as well as the sightseeing, hotel, and travel arrangements. In addition, this team had bonded intensely, so asking them to write offered all of us closure.

Much to their delight, the boys were asked to write on their paper airsickness bags. The assignment: Share three things you liked on the trip and three things that could be changed or eliminated. The boys' lists were informative and at times pretty funny. Many players made quick lists; others wrote extensively on both sides of the bags. Those writings—which I still possess—got me thinking, and my thoughts morphed into Team Notebooks and Athletes' Journals, a fairly inglorious beginning, to be sure.

The Basic Team Notebook

The notebooks really helped my coaching . . . the players were able to put voice to their frustrations and concerns. They were also able to objectively view what they did well and focus on what needed to be improved. The sheets did assist in open communication between coaching staff and players.

–Matt Grawrock, Head Coach, Southern Virginia University

The basic team notebook introduced in this book contains five sections:

- Preseason Thoughts
- Competition Analysis I
- Competition Analysis II
- Postseason Thoughts
- Athletes' Notes

The following are brief explanations of the basic five sections using templates from my former high school soccer program. While reading these sheets from soccer, think about how you will adapt them for your sport.

- *Preseason Thoughts:* The prompts on this page (Figure 1.1, soccer) help athletes think about the previous season and the upcoming season. Athletes write about their preparation and goals for the season. Writing Preseason Thoughts takes the average athlete 10–15 minutes. Depending on the number of athletes, a coach will read and perhaps take notes on the collection in 15 to 30 minutes.
- *Competition Analysis I:* The prompts on this page (Figure 1.2, soccer) help athletes reflect on a game or match. The one-page reflection takes an average player 3–5 minutes to complete. Depending on the number of athletes, coaches will read and perhaps take notes on the collection in 10–20 minutes.
- *Competition Analysis II:* The prompts on this page (Figure 1.3, soccer) assist athletes in writing about a game that a team watches together. The two-page observation takes athletes approximately 10 minutes to complete and may be used as a discussion guide. Coaches may read and perhaps take notes on the collection in 10–20 minutes.
- *Postseason Thoughts:* The prompts on this page (Figure 1.4, soccer) help players in thinking about the past season while

Preseason Thoughts

Player: ______________ Grade: _____ Phone: ________________________
Email: ______________ Address: ______________________________________
Parents/Guardians: ____
Phone(s): __________ Email of Parents/Guardians: _____________________

- My strengths last year as a player:

- My weaknesses last year as a player:

- My preparation for this season has been the following:

- My goals for this season include the following:

- Last year our team strengths included:

- Last year our team weaknesses included:

- I am taking the following classes this fall:

- Other thoughts:

Figure 1.1 Preseason Thoughts (soccer)

Competition Analysis I

Player: ______________

Falcons v. _________ Date: _______ Place: _________ Final Score: _______

Records: Falcons: __W __L __D Opponent: __W __L __D

- My strengths as a player in today's match:
- My weaknesses as a player in today's match:
- Team strengths in today's match:
- Team weaknesses in today's match:
- Opponent's strengths:
- Opponent's weaknesses:
- What was the "difference" in today's match:
- What team adjustment would you suggest for the next match against this opponent?
- Other comments about team strategy, attitude, preparation. . . .

Figure 1.2 Competition Analysis I (soccer)

Competition Analysis II

Player: ______________

Team #1____________	Team #2 ____________
Alignment of Players: ________	Alignment of Players: ________
Team Strengths:	Team Strengths:
Team Weaknesses:	Team Weaknesses:
Half-time adjustments:	Half-time adjustments:

General Comments:

Forwards	Forwards
Midfielders	Midfielders
Defenders	Defenders
Keeper	Keeper
Man of the Match: Player ______________	*Man of the Match*: Player ______________
Why?	Why?

Describe the Moment of the Match:

Your Final Analysis:
Think as a coach about team strengths and/or weaknesses (e.g., athleticism, speed, coaching, motivation/heart). What adjustments might you have made to either team if you were that team's coach? (Use the back of the page.)

Figure 1.3 Competition Analysis II (soccer)

Postseason Reflections

Player:_______________

- My strengths this season as a player:

- My weaknesses this season as a player:

- In the off-season here's what I plan to do to improve as a player for the next season:

- When I review the goals I set for myself at the beginning of the season in my notebook, here is how I think I did:

- This year our team strengths included:

- This year our team weaknesses included:

- Here's how I am doing in my classes this season:

Class:	How I'm Doing:
-	
-	
-	
-	
-	

- Other thoughts:

Figure 1.4 Postseason Reflections (soccer)

Figure 1.5 Back page of Notes (Sport: soccer)

making plans for the future. As with Preseason Thoughts, an athlete may take 15–20 minutes to write out these thoughts and a coach may read and perhaps take notes on the collection in 15–30 minutes.

- *Athlete's Notes:* These pages are for keeping notes, sketching plays, and storing information like handouts from the coach. The pages may be blank pieces of paper or the coach (or players) may create any number of different page styles. See Figure 1.5 for one example of a soccer notes page where players may take notes or sketch plays. Also in this section, for travel or select teams, a coach might include directions to venues as well as background information on the teams to be watched, schools to be played, or tourist sights to be seen.

Inside Team Notebooks

When Amy Edwards served as associate head coach for the University of Missouri women's soccer team, Team Notebooks were implemented after she read three of my articles in *Soccer Journal* (Kent, 2008). At the conclusion of Missouri's 2008 season, Coach Edwards sent me an email to debrief their season with Team Notebooks. In the first paragraph she wrote,

> I wanted to update you on our use of Team Notebooks as well as how our season ended up. . . . First, we used the *Preseason Thoughts* and *Match Analysis I* primarily. I also incorporated a *Pre/Post Game Sheets* that asked [players] to identify how they prepared for the game as far as nutritionally, physically, and mentally. This gave both the coaches and players great insight on how their preparation was affecting their performance. We are very concerned about recovery from Friday to Sunday games so that really helped make it a priority for the players as well. With the use of the *Match Analysis I* . . . we were able to address issues individually that we would not be aware of otherwise. It was also such a great learning tool for the players. As much as they didn't want to admit it, they enjoyed reflecting overall. I truly believe it had a huge positive impact on our success. Our team had never been so in tune with themselves as well as taking ownership of their team and destiny.

As a researcher, I valued Coach Edwards' detailed observations of her team's use of the notebooks. She alludes to key themes in my studies and identified facets of writing to learn in athletics, including the ways

- athletes prepare for competition,
- writing can affect performance,
- written reflection about an experience can help athletes learn more about that experience,
- athletes become more in tune with themselves and their teammates,
- writing can help athletes take responsibility for their performances, good or bad, and
- a coach's insight into practices and performances may be enhanced.

As a coach, I admired how Edwards adapted the Team Notebook concept to fit her program's needs by creating "*Pre/Post Game Sheets* that asked [players] to identify how they prepared for the game as far as nutritionally, physically, and mentally." The coach's professional initiative and creativity serve as an instructive tool to us all. In her email's final paragraph, Edwards highlights the University of Missouri team's accomplishments:

> We had the most successful season in program history. We broke numerous records. We won the Big 12 Tournament, made it to the 2nd round of the NCAA's, finished up with our highest RPI ranking ever, best season record ever 16–5–2. We are taking a trip to Brazil in a few days with the team. I plan to have [the players write] the postseason sheet and use the Match Analysis II for the pro game we will be attending. I want to put the Team Notebook into full force with our program.

Now the head coach at Gonzaga University, Coach Amy Edwards has also implemented Team Notebooks with her *Zags*.

Andy Stills

Obviously, Team Notebooks don't guarantee a championship season. But those of us involved in athletics know that the difference between being a champion or landing one step down on the podium can be figured in hundredths of seconds or a quarter inch here or there. Likewise, athletic improvement, as Andy recognized when writing in his Preseason Thoughts, can be realized in a few extra minutes a day of practice:

> Last year you made us write about our preparation for the season. One thing I wrote about was foul shooting. My sophomore year I took 50 foul shots at home most every day. When I wrote you I realized that 50 foul shots added up to like 20,000 foul shots a year. I went up to 75 this year and now its 30,000! Like you always say coach it's about *court time.*

I'd like to end this small story saying that Andy hit the winning foul shot in a championship game. He didn't. But his foul shooting percentage did improve and he recognized more fully the value of practice as he wrote in his Postseason Thoughts:

> Check it out, coach. My foul shooting % went up 15 points!
> Quote in our notebooks: "There is no glory in practice, but without practice, there is no glory." Glory be to practice!!!

Helping our athletes recognize the cause-and-effect realities of practice remains forever a critical goal of effective coaching. Writing is one way to achieve that goal. And yes, Andy, "Glory be to practice . . ."

Adapting Team Notebooks for Your Program

You may decide to add or delete sections of the basic Team Notebook to fit your specific program needs. As noted, Coach Edwards created Pre/Post Game Sheets (Figure 1.6) to help her athletes think more about game preparation and recovery. In the NCAA Division I soccer world "recovery from Friday to Sunday games" is a critical issue. As Edwards explained, the Pre/Post Game Sheets "gave both the coaches and players great insight on how their preparation was affecting their performance."

Baseball coach Jim Dawber of Rhode Island added the Team Notebook sections to materials he had gathered over his coaching career and created a Players' Instructional Manual. He included a weekly Personal Evaluation Checklist, a weekly Team Report Card, a Quality At-Bat Card, and pages of advice on hitting, pitching, fielding, focus, and motivation. I admire his Quality-At-Bat Card (Figure 1.7), an idea Jim modified from an article in *Collegiate Baseball Weekly* "to fit the language and teaching" he uses with his players. The QAB Card asks his players to reflect on their batting immediately after a game. Dawber's Players' Instructional Manual, nearly one hundred pages long, certainly lets his players know that they have stepped into a serious and studious program.

When at Temple University, lacrosse coach Nicole Moore helped to institute Team Notebooks. The Temple staff added a page to help athletes think about recovery following an injury (Figure 1.8). The page kept trainers and coaches informed of athletes' rehab plans. In addition, the Temple staff created a PreGame Thoughts page as illustrated in Figure 1.9. Notice the intensity within Jen Homka's writing as she prepares for the first game of the season.

For the travel teams that I coached, adding day-by-day journal pages helped the teenaged players keep track of their activities. This journal, plus a follow-up trip letter from me, offered the players' parents a sense of their sons' or daughters' tour. With the addition of this page, the Team Notebook served as both a learning tool and scrapbook of the trip.

Name: *Gonzaga #18* Opponent: *Pepperdine* Date: *Friday*

Pregame Mental Preparation:
Visualization—scoring goals—pressing once ball is lost
Positive self talk while going over individual and team goals
Watch individual highlight video
Read over opponent scouting report

Pregame Nutritional Preparation:
Hydrated day before the game
A handful of Hershey Kisses before the game—Caffeine
Snack—Almonds
Pregame meal—Chicken Breast, salad, + fruit

Pregame Physical Preparation:
Ice bath day before the game
Dynamic warm-up + stretch
Loose pregame warm-up

Post game Mental Evaluation and Recovery:
Fill out post-game match analysis
Set goals for next game
Watched Friends episodes

Post game Nutritional Recovery:
Muscle Milk
Chicken Salad—post game meal
Water

Post game Physical Recovery:
Stretch routine
Ice bath
Dynamic movement recovery swim

Figure 1.6 Pre/Post Game Sheets, Gonzaga University Women's Soccer

Cumberland High School Baseball

Quality-At-Bat Card

Evaluate yourself on the process—what you do control—rather than the outcome (results)—what is outside of your control!

Name: ____________________ Date: ____________________

Opponent: __________________ Talent level(s) [A–D]: ______

Tough questions for a Mentally-Tough Player

Did I study the pitcher from the dugout? _____

Did I use my routine? _____

Did I have a clear, simple plan on each pitch? _____

Was I committed to the plan or did I just go through the motions? _____

Did I trust myself, or was I anxious and jump out at the ball? _____

Was I under control? Did I use the Composure Drill when I started to 'lose it'? _____

Was I Focused? Did I use a Focal Point or the Trash Can Drill to assist me? _____

Number of Plate Appearances _____

Emotionally in control of myself _____

Had a plan and stuck to it _____

Saw the ball well _____

Made solid contact _____

Base hits _____

Overall Quality-At-Bats _____

Be in, and stay in, control of yourself. Breathe deep and relax.
Trust your hands. Trust your plan. Trust yourself.

Figure 1.7 Quality-At-Bat Card (Coach Jim Dawber)

Temple Lacrosse

Injury Rehabilitation Thoughts

Player: ______________ Date: _________ Trainer: ______________

Projected Rehab Time:

Goals for practice:

Goals for weight room:

Rehab Plan and Timeline:

What can I do for my teammates and coaches through my rehab program:

How am I going to take care of MYSELF through my rehab program:

What I would like to improve on through my rehab program:

My goals for my injury rehab include the following:

Other thoughts:

Figure 1.8 Temple Lacrosse Injury Rehabilitation Thoughts

Temple Lacrosse
PreGame Thoughts

Player: Jennifer Lynn Marie Homka
Date: 02/20/2010

My FEELINGS on the upcoming games are:
I am looking forward to the upcoming game because I am very anxious and ready to get the season started with a win!! I am also a little bit nervous since it is our first real game as a team since the fall, but I am willing to give it my all to get the team pumped and ready to win.

My THOUGHTS on the upcoming game are:
I am wondering what types of plays they run this year if any, or if there are any key players we have to watch for. Also, how they work on transition defense for us to get the ball moving up field. I believe that our offense has a lot of talent and are ready to play against good competition. Though I believe we need to keep the ball moving whether it is a free lance or a play and work the ball around while staying spread out and not bunch in the 8 meter. As for defense I feel like we are doing a decent job with the USA defense. I feel like if we talk (communicate) and slide to help each other we will be unstoppable. Also, I feel like as long as we move the ball up the field on transition without freaking out or throwing the ball away we will not turn the ball over. I do feel though that since it is out first game of the season that some people will be nervous.

What OUR TEAM has been doing to prepare for the upcoming game has been:
We have been practicing, conditioning, and watching videos of our practices and other games to find things we do good and things we need to work on. We have been working on our offensive plays and different types of defense. We worked on transitions both recovering and going up the field.

What I have been doing to prepare for the upcoming game has been:
Practicing, conditioning, working hard in practice to get the most out of it, though a couple days this week I was struggling with pain in the knee that was hard to play my best. I have been thinking about this game for weeks and the closer it gets the more excited I am to see how we are against a decent team. I have also been talking with teammates trying to get them pumped and trying to help them with little things that could help their play. I feel like we are ready to get this season on the way.

What I think OUR TEAM will bring on game day:
I think our team will bring competitiveness, positive attitudes, and anxiousness to see what it is like this season for us. I think we all will bring it all and do the best we can. I think we all will be there for each other in support either on the field or on the sideline.

Figure 1.9 PreGame Thoughts, Temple University Women's Lacrosse *(continued)*

What I think I will bring on game day:
On game day I will bring myself ready to play my best and hardest. I want to leave it all out on the field and do not hold anything back. I will make sure my mind and body are ready for everything. I will be there to help my teammates with anything that is needed. I planned to do whatever I am told to do and to do it the best possible way.

What I think our opponent in the upcoming game will bring:
I think Rutgers will bring intensity and their best skills possible. They are an aggressive team so we need to be ready for everything. Rutgers will be throwing a lot of competition at us and we need to stay composed and not freak out if something goes wrong. I am sure they will have plays to run against us and we need to be ready for it. They are a quick team.

What I WILL DO from this point on to PREPARE for the upcoming game:
I will mentally and physically think about what I need to do for myself and for my team. I need to work hard to make sure my skills are sharp and ready for any and all action. I will continue to watch videos and think about the game until it comes. I am so excited for game day!

What I WILL DO for my team to help us all PREPARE for the upcoming game:
What I will do for my team to help us all prepare is to push not only myself every day, but also my teammates. I will make them work hard to give it all they got whether it is a competitive groundball or crashing a stop, etc. I will get everybody ready also mentally thinking about the game and what we need to bring to the game. We need to start the season off right.

What I will need to do to PREPARE MENTALLY for the upcoming game:
Mentally, I need to think about what I am going to do to help myself and my teammates. What am I going to do right and try to fix if something isn't sharp. What we need to do as a team and on the defensive end. Communicating with all my teammates and coaches! Be assertive and ready to take action at whatever comes at me.

What I will need to do to PREPARE PHYSICALLY for the upcoming game:
Work hard and go after every ball possible. Make sure my stick skills are sharp and ready for any action. Have my legs ready to move in any and all directions for defense. And whatever else I can do to get myself physically ready. The day before I will make sure I have enough sleep, energy, and fuel in my body.

Other thoughts:
LET'S DO THIS TU!!! GAMMEEEE DAYYY SOOOO SOOONNNNN!!!

GO OWLS!!!!

Figure 1.9 *(continued)*

Perhaps players need to think more about the connection of training sessions to competitions. Create a new Team Notebook section of writing prompts focused on practice sessions and use them periodically. Maybe a coach needs to get a better handle on players' academic standings. Develop a report card that players and their teachers fill out. Other sections such as the following may be added, too:

- *Journal Prompts* that help athletes look more closely at themselves as competitors, students, and people:
  - When you were young, whom did you admire as an athlete and why?
  - Whom do you now admire as an athlete and why?
  - What makes a good training partner?
  - What makes an effective coach?
  - Other than a coach, who brings out the best in you as an athlete and why?
- *Quotable Quotes Pages* that offer athletes a place to keep a list of interesting and/or comical who-said-what's from the athletic season.
- *Blank Pages* that give athletes a place to include newspaper clippings or photographs.

Adding more sections creates opportunities for more activities and deeper learning, and transforms Team Notebooks into a workbook for the season. But, adding more sections can add more time. That decision is yours. Always keep in mind that the most effective Team Notebook is the one that works for you and your program. Here's what worked for me as a high school soccer coach.

My Team Notebooks

With my high school soccer team, I used the basic five-section Team Notebook and depending on team needs, I sometimes added other sections or activities. I taught in a small high school of 500 students, and at one time or another I "coached" most of my players in English class, too. As a result, these student-athletes were accustomed to writing, so none seemed especially surprised or bothered when I introduced writing as a soccer activity. The basic Team Notebook also worked well with select travel teams.

- My high school Team Notebooks included the following:
  - *Cover Page*
  - *Coach's Letter*
  - *Preseason Thoughts*
  - *Competition Analysis I* (18 copies)
  - *Competition Analysis II* (5 copies)
  - *Postseason Thoughts*
  - *Quotable Quotes*
  - *Notes Pages*
  - *Brief Program History*
- My State Travel Team Notebooks included the following:
  - *Cover Page*
  - *Coach's Letter*
  - *Collection of Quotations from Player Profiles*
  - *Day-by-day Journal*
  - *Competition Analysis I*
  - *Competition Analysis II* (for professional matches we attended)
  - *Notes Pages*
  - *Informational Pages* (e.g., English Football League standings; London Underground Map; emergency numbers and contacts.)

The following will help with organizing of the notebooks:

- Purchase three-ring binders from a discount office store for each member of the team. On the cover print and attach the player's name along with the school's name and mascot. Players often decorate their own covers.
- Photocopy each section of the notebook on different colored paper. Our school's photocopy machine automatically punched three holes in the paper so use that feature.

- To keep up with the fourteen to eighteen *Competition Analysis I* my players wrote per season, I asked them to fill out the sheet right after a match. Occasionally, a player wanted to spend more time writing and asked to take it home; that usually didn't cause a problem. My best advice, however, is to collect the sheet immediately following the competition.
- I enjoyed and learned from reading my players' notebook pages. Therefore, I read them as soon as I could. Even after a night game, when I got home I read my kids' reflections. A few times some of the entries warranted a phone call to check in on a player. And at practice, some of their entries gave me a place to start up a necessary conversation (e.g., when a player has been performing poorly and losing playing time).
- I made copies of my players' completed sheets. Some years an assistant coach or a manager copied the pages. Some years I did it.
- We didn't copy the players' *Notes* sections. I did ask them to pass in their top one or two *Quotable Quotes* so I could use them during the end-of-the-year banquet. Sometimes, I gave away an award for the best quotation of the season.
- Travel Team Notebooks were soft covered and depending on the length of the tour may have had fewer pages. I didn't make copies of the pages during the tour, but at some point I collected all the notebooks and read through them when convenient.
- As far as the time involved in using Team Notebooks, I never found them time intensive. Could a coach lower the time involved and still provide a beneficial learning experience? Absolutely. Use the Preseason and Postseason Thoughts; try out a Competition Analysis I for one-third of the games; and use the Competition Analysis II for one game. So, a condensed Team Notebook would look like this:
    - *Cover Page*
    - *Coach's Note*
    - *Preseason Thoughts*
    - *Competition Analysis I* (5)
    - *Competition Analysis II* (1)

- *Notes Pages*
- *Postseason Thoughts*

Again, do what's best for your team and program.

Learning Styles: One Theory That Supports the Use of Team Notebooks

Everything we do in life is rooted in theory.

—bell hooks

Think about your current team and how your athletes are different. Take music, for example: Some love reggae, others the "oldies." Once in while you probably have an athlete who listens to Bach. In terms of learning, our athletes are different, too.

Howard Gardner's *Theory of Multiple Intelligences* (Gardner, 1983, 1993) is as true for the playing field as it is for the science or English classroom. "According to Howard Gardner, human beings have nine different kinds of intelligence that reflect different ways of interacting with the world. Each person has a unique combination, or profile. Although we each have all nine intelligences, no two individuals have them in the same exact configuration—similar to our fingerprints" (PBS Educational Resources). In athletics, the predominant intelligences may be "bodily-kinesthetic," "spatial," and "Linguistic intelligence." Review Figure 1.10 and see if you agree.

Consider, for example, how college-level athletes may learn about an opponent. Figure 1.11 presents various information sources available to athletes and coaches. Think of the ways that the writing from the pages in a Team Notebook could enhance learning by using the players'

- *Competition Analysis I* from a previous game as a study guide for an upcoming game with the same opponent,
- *Competition Analysis II* after watching a match film of an opponent, and
- *Notes* page to sketch the opponent's system of play.

Such activities not only enhance learning, but they also create unique opportunities to provide more variety to practice sessions, add to pregame discussions, and frontload post-match debriefings.

Gardner's Theory of Multiple Intelligences as Applied to Athletics

Logical–Mathematical: This intelligence focuses on reasoning. Logical--mathematical athletes show strengths in organizing, questioning, calculating, and experimenting; they're good at solving puzzles and learning facts. You might find these athletes volunteering to do statistics for the team or organizing a team history page for the notebook.

Spatial–Visual: This intelligence focuses on pictures and images. Spatial–visual student-athletes could be your artsy athletes who show talent in illustrating, drawing, sketching; they love graphics or producing videos. You might find these athletes drawing or sketching plays or new formations with a friend.

Naturalist: This intelligence focuses on the natural world. Naturalist student-athletes are connected to the outdoors and enjoy astronomy, meteorology, long walks in the woods, and exploring. These athletes may love a rainy-day game or find indoor chalk-talk sessions difficult to endure.

Linguistic–Verbal: This intelligence focuses on the use of words. Linguistic–verbal athletes enjoy language through writing, reading, speaking, and interpreting. These athletes may be the ones who readily speak up during team discussions, write a lot in their Team Notebooks, keep their own journals, or enjoy writing on the team's Facebook page or blog.

Interpersonal: This intelligence focuses on communicating with other people. These athletes have people skills and may end up being a team captain. They may also chat-up officials. Coaches readily place recruits with student-athletes who have strong interpersonal intelligence because they are never at a loss of words and enjoy talking with others.

Musical–Rhythmic: This intelligence focuses on melodies and rhythms. My musical–rhythmic athletes love to sing, play instruments, and listen to music on their iPods. I had one high school soccer team that enjoyed singing so much that we started a chorus at the high school called The Varsity Singers (at first, members had to have a varsity letter, but that soon changed). One travel team that loved to sing ended up in a London Underground station (subway) singing to the commuters and tourists. The athletes held up signs: "US Soccer Team Robbed: Need Money to Get Home." In fact, many of our dormitory rooms had been pilfered, but we had our airline tickets and enough money for the tour. I'm sure those boys will never forget singing in the

Figure 1.10 Theory of Multiple Intelligences (adapted from PBS Educational Resources, n.d.) *(continued)*

station and having friendly Londoners toss money at them—but then, of course, along came the bobbies . . .

Intrapersonal: This intelligence focuses on reflective thinking. Those student-athletes who prosper within this intelligence are in touch with their own feelings. They enjoy self-assessing and quiet moments of reflection. These athletes may not be as rah-rah as some of their teammates and like their Linguistic–Verbal counterparts, they may write a lot on their Team Notebook pages or within their Athletes' Journals.

Bodily–Kinesthetic: This intelligence focuses on bodily movements. Obviously, many of your athletes live for this intelligence.

Existential Intelligence: the ability and proclivity to pose (and ponder) questions about life, death, and ultimate realities. On long flights, in hotel rooms, or on the endless rides on the yellow bus, our existential athletes and their big questions always surface.

Figure 1.10 (*continued*)

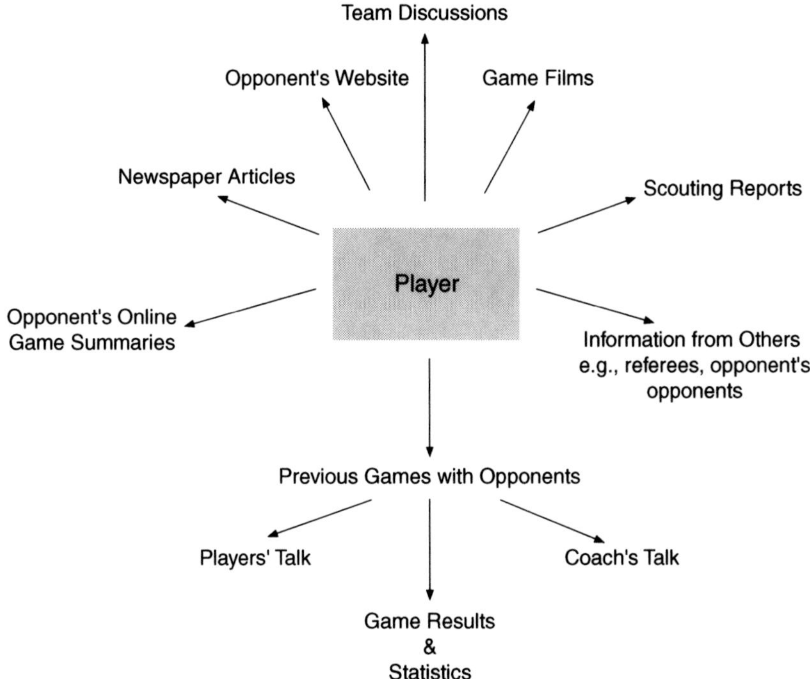

Figure 1.11 Ways Athletes Learn about an Opponent

And so . . .

Over the years Team Notebooks became as important to my coaching as watching game films and as much a part of my players' learning as attending university matches. Writing guided my players in thinking more critically about the full spectrum of their sport. In essence, writing helped my athletes think and talk more like coaches. With Team Notebooks to complement my coaching practice, I knew I was looking more seriously than ever before at my teams, athletes, and coaching. Indeed, the notion of writing to learn in athletics encouraged me—and my athletes—to live more fully as students of the game.

Chapter Two

Preseason Thoughts: Looking Back, Thinking Forward, and Making Plans

The first order of reality on a team is the athlete's point of view.
–adapted from Vivian Paley, teacher

Coming to Know Our Athletes

When friends ask about those trips to England, I smirk and say, "Thirteen years. Thirty teams. Five hundred players. Seven arrests." And yes, all seven of the license-plate bandits were released into my custody . . . at two o'clock in the morning on the last day of the tour.

The athletes selected for these teams lived all across the state of Maine, and in most cases we did not know each other. Player Profile sheets (Figure 2.1) mailed out months before leaving helped the players think about the trip, their soccer, and their roles on the team while helping me come to know the athletes I'd be coaching. Excerpts from a goalkeeper's profile provide good examples:

Attach Photo Here

The Maine Team

Player Profile

Name ____________________ School ______________ Grade____ Age ______

Address ____________________ (Town) ______________ (Zip) ____________

Parent/Guardian Names____

Phones _________ (H) __________ (C) Height____ Weight _________________

Years Played ____ Position______ Alternate Position _______________________

Hometown Newspaper_______________ Regional Newspaper _______________

Please describe your strengths & areas needing improvement as a soccer player:

____

____

____

____

____

____

List any Honors that you have received as a student-athlete:

____

____

High School Coach ____________________ Phone _________________

ODP or Club Coach ____________________ Phone _________________

Other Sports ____

Other activities ____

Post Graduation Plans ____

Have you travel overseas before? ____ Where? ___________________________

On the back of this form, please describe yourself as a person and player. What makes you happy? Sad? Angry? Is there anything you're concerned about with respect to this team and tour?

Figure 2.1 Player Profile Sheets (Maine Team)

> *Please describe yourself. What makes you happy? Sad? Angry? Anything make you nervous about this team and the tour?*
> To start off I am happy to have been chosen for the opportunity to play for the Maine Team. I'm also excited to travel to England and enjoy the experience (soccer & culture wise). I am however sketchy about the plane ride . . . w/my luck [someone will] bomb or hijack the plane the team is on. (Thought I would tell someone!) Also I'm worried about the competition from England, how good will they be? Will I be good enough?
>
> *Please describe your strengths & areas needing improvement as a soccer player:*
> My weaknesses are procrastination and staying in constant shape. Also I sometimes show low self-esteem. My strengths are my commitment to soccer, my quest to be the best, and my enthusiasm.
>
> —Joshua Verville

Joshua's clear-cut answers on the Player Profile made me feel confident in this young man as both person and player. I knew from the recommendation by his high school coach that Joshua was a talented goalkeeper; his writing assured me that he was also a thoughtful person.

From each of the Player Profiles, I selected one or two lines to include in a collection (Figure 2.2) with the players and other team personnel. I mailed the collection in the next set of pre-trip letters and also placed the list at the front of the Team Notebook. Notice while reading "What You Said" how the words have the potential to ease athlete anxiety while creating pathways for discussion. Also, from what you have read in Joshua's writing above, you can see how Player Profiles helped me learn more about these athletes as people.

These travel team Player Profiles served as forerunners to Preseason Thoughts. Although the two documents' prompts are not exactly the same, they both provide athletes space to reflect and coaches opportunities to learn about their players.

Preseason Thoughts

The prompts provided in Preseason Thoughts (Figure 2.3) not only guide athletes in reflection, but also help establish a team-wide tone of thoughtful inquiry. As the chapter title suggests, we look back to think about the previous season and the off-season in an effort to plan forward

Maine Team '94

"What You Said . . ."

- I'm a little nervous about flying on a plane since I never have.
- One thing that makes me nervous about this trip is how rough English soccer is.
- I'm psyched to see the pro games . . .
- How good will the teams we're playing be? Will I be good enough?
- I see myself as a pretty nice person.
- I guess you could say I'm an athletic, laid-back kid who loves soccer.
- All I can say is that I can't wait to play on this team.
- I guess I'm your typical teenager trying to get through high school.
- For the most part I can get along with any personality and I hope that's true about The Maine Team.
- (Almost) a fear I have is that people will have a bad impression of me.
- I love to meet new people.
- I'm a pretty relaxed person . . .
- To tell you the truth, I wonder how I'll match up against the English kids.
- My least favorite thing in life is homework.
- I'm a bit nervous about the plane ride . . .
- I like skiing, hunting, fishing, basketball, and obviously soccer.
- Selfish players make me angry.
- Guys who think they're GREAT make me sick.
- Meeting new people and playing English teams make me a little nervous.
- I don't mind shopping (if it's my parents' money).
- I heard you, Coach Kent, are a soccer god. [This quote is my personal favorite! CK]
- I'm psyched to represent the state.
- I'm looking forward to meeting my teammates and kicking a little butt with you, Coach.
- I want to sit on the corner in London some place and just take it in.
- I've been thinking, this is once in a lifetime, isn't it?
- Thanks for everything so far, Coach. I can't wait!

Figure 2.2 "What You Said" Collection from Maine Team players

Falcon Soccer
Preseason Thoughts

Player: Jonathan Grade: 11 | Phone: 364.2953
Email: *jonathan@email.com* | Address: *Porter Avenue West*
Parents/Guardians: *Rylee and Christian*
Phone: 364.2953 Cell: 416.8111 | Parent/Guardian Email: *home@email.com*

- **My strengths last year as a player:**
  Last year I felt confident in the air. I loved winning 50–50 balls. I've gained a lot of confidence on the pitch these past couple of years. I understand the game better—I can see how attacks are developing and I know what to say to my defenders. I bet if you asked the forwards from other teams they'd say I'm good at delaying. I love playing against great players (Remington from Telstar)—I used to get scared, now I get up for them.

- **My weaknesses last year as a player:**
  My communication wasn't the best. Like you said, young players think about themselves & don't talk much—experienced players speak up. Thanks to the summer matches I already have better talk. My left foot was squirrely . . . Not this year! ☺

- **My preparation for this season has been the following:**
  Winter soccer, summer matches, and camp. I coached community center summer soccer. I did the deal! I'm prepared. Bring it on.

- **My goals for this season include the following:**
  Talk, composure, & leadership on and off the pitch.

- **Last year our team strengths included:**
  Moving to space. Staying composed during physical matches. We liked each other!

- **Last year our team weaknesses included:**
  What can I say, we were young. Not really a weakness but like you said our age defined our play. We didn't have the strength to finish a lot of our attacks. Not this year! Light it up!

- **I am taking the following classes this fall:**
  Physics
  Pre-Calculus
  Writing Center English
  US History
  Psychology

- **Other thoughts:**
  I'm psyched we have friendlies against Class A teams like Lewiston—playing up will help us.
  I know it's a pain → BUT, everyone likes the spaghetti feeds at your house. The first 11 will help with clean up and everything.
  I guarantee we'll make it through the second round of the play-offs this year. We're ready.

Figure 2.3 Jonathan's Preseason Thoughts

toward the season at hand. In the final prompt, "Other Thoughts," athletes often write about whatever is uppermost in their minds, athletic or not.

Having our athletes stop and reflect on the new sports season makes good sense, but getting there . . . ? As a novice coach, I wanted to help my players to set goals and think about the upcoming season. The results from my players back then ended up very much like Mark Jackson's, a high school football coach from California.

Mark passed out paper and pens after the first practice and asked his players to write their goals for the season. One wrote, "I want to score six touchdowns and go to homecoming with a cheerleader." Other players' responses ran the gamut, including my personal favorite "I want a cool picture of me in the newspaper so I can show my kids some day." Like Mark, my what-are-your-goals-for-the-season question didn't extend my players' thinking in meaningful ways. In effect, they wrote, I read, and we moved on with our preseason practices and games.

In time, I developed this more comprehensive collection of prompts that became Preseason Thoughts. Responding to these prompts assisted my athletes in unpacking their thinking, and as a result, extended their knowledge and awareness about our training, match play, and the team. In addition, this activity set a tone focused on learning.

Setting the Tone

Kicking-off the sports season with well-crafted training sessions, a range of team-building activities, and a variety of educational activities does, indeed, set a tone for the season. On our team, the senior players organized two-day training camps at my family's lakeside cabins. A white-sand beach and spring-fed lake provided the backdrop for all-day practice sessions and discussions about the season.

Coaches also invite outside presenters like physical therapists, nutritionists, and former star athletes from our own programs to teach our athletes and maintain that tone. Sport psychologist Dr. Rob Ferguson, a former alpine ski athlete and team captain, spoke to our fifty-five ski racers about mental training for anxiety control. The talk included exercises for centering and visualization training. Together, we created a phrase that our ski athletes returned to repeatedly during the season: "See the course, ski the course." Back then, I didn't use Team Notebooks per se, but I know that they would have fit right in with our ski team's activities.

Organization

Preseason Thoughts may be handed out in a hardcopy format at a preseason meeting or at the first training session of the season. If you send an information packet to an athlete's home, Preseason Thoughts may be included with a self-addressed-stamped envelope for return. Always include a due date for return and remind athletes to print legibly and, if copies of the pages will be kept, to use black or blue ink to insure quality photocopying.

The time it takes an athlete to write Preseason Thoughts varies from 10 to 15 minutes. The lengths vary, too, as some athletes will dash off their responses while others will ponder each question and write more extensively. Expect a few athletes to email or call, asking, "Coach, is this what you want? Is this right?" Simply remind them that you're looking for their thoughts.

I return the original copies immediately and on those occasions that I am compelled to highlight or make notes, I write only on the photocopies. Why? I believe that my writing in their notebooks has the tendency to influence their thinking the next time they write. Naturally, my influence as coach is bound to be there in one way or another, but as much as possible I want my athletes' notebooks to be theirs.

Not everyone agrees with me about writing back to athletes in their notebooks or journals. Former high school soccer coach Rick Jacobs did write back to his players as a way to show concern, offer advice, and build relationships (personal interview, June 19, 2008). Now vice president of operations for Major League Soccer's Philadelphia Union, Jacobs is the all-time leader in winning percentage among American high school coaches (94 percent) according to the National Soccer Coaches Association of America. His St. Benedict's teams won six national titles and compiled a 519-27-13 record during Jacobs's 25-year career.

Using Technology

Some coaches utilize email, team websites, social networks, blogs, GoogleDocs, and other online programs to share news, announcements, and photos. The prompts for Preseason Thoughts may be included on these sites for athletes to access. If a coach likes the idea of an online approach but doesn't have the expertise, a tech-savvy assistant coach or player will be able to help. Popular these days are free online spreadsheets and surveys that may be used with athletes. They're simple and insure an athlete's privacy. Also, you don't have to worry about reading poor handwriting. Most schools and universities provide similar platforms (e.g., Moodle, Blackboard) if you choose to use an online format.

Record Keeping

I keep the photocopies of the notebook sheets in large three-ring binders. The binders are divided into five sections. If you choose to go digital, you will store your players' writing in a computer-based format. Either format allows for quick reading; however, the online format can save you time by allowing you to copy and paste pieces of an athlete's writing to use in recommendations or, if like Coach Jacobs, you wanted to write back to your athletes.

Uses for the Coach

When I read the collection of Preseason Thoughts, I come to know the team's view of the previous season and how individual athletes prepared for this one. Their writing also provides a snapshot of the team's attitude and frame of mind. Of course, it is just a snapshot, one moment in time, but we have to start somewhere. For a coach, as with a classroom teacher, the first order of reality on a team is the athlete's point of view (as adapted from Paley, 1981). Indeed, we have to start where our athletes are, not where we hope or think they should be, and build from there. Ultimately, and perhaps most important of all, the writing from Preseason Thoughts promotes an even deeper relationship between my athletes and me.

Preseason Thoughts can be helpful when I write players' recommendations. When possible, I quote players directly from their Preseason Thoughts. In Jonathan's Preseason Thoughts, he addresses his "Talk, composure, & leadership on and off the pitch." Coupled with my own observations of his maturity and leadership abilities, the recommendation takes on a richer, more thorough quality.

Our reading of Preseason Thoughts, or any of the Team Notebook pages, improves with experience. Here's some of my thinking focused on Jonathan's writing in his Preseason Thoughts:

How to Read Preseason Thoughts: A Closer Look

Jonathan's writing reveals an 11th grader who has prepared well for the soccer season. On the pitch and in the classroom, this 16-year-old shows himself to be a thoughtful young man. Your team has its Jonathans or JoAnnas, too. His balanced personality and steady play bring calm and confidence to his fellow defenders and, indeed, to the whole team.

What's striking about Jonathan's writing is how well he sees himself as a soccer player. Notice the specifics he uses to write about himself:

> "I felt confident in the air [heading the ball last year]."
> "I can see how attacks are developing and I know what to say to my defenders."
> "I'm good at delaying [the opponents as they attack]."
> "[Last year] my communication wasn't the best."
> "My left foot was squirrely [inconsistent] . . . Not this year! ☺"

He writes with the kind of knowledge and understanding that next-level players possess; he identifies his strengths and challenges in a way that a coach would speak about a player. And still, Jonathan's writing is that of a fun-loving teenager who's all about the game, his friends, and spaghetti feeds at the coach's.

When reading the photocopies of my players' Preseason Thoughts, I sometimes use a highlighter to note certain passages (e.g., when a player has a part-time job). Even though I know my high school players fairly well, I always discover something through this reading. For example, on Jonathan's page he writes that he intends to provide "leadership on and off the pitch." When I read that this young man saw himself as a leader off the pitch in arenas like school and the community, I felt I might have captain material in Jonathan, and indeed I did. Such statements from players make great talking points if you arrange individual meetings with athletes. Like many coaches, I spend a lot of productive time on the bus speaking with my players, assistant, and trainer. Using comments from Team Notebook sheets to initiate or move discussions forward has been helpful.

A junior in high school, Jonathan is a next-level player who's genuinely dedicated. He writes that he has prepared for the season by participating in "[w]inter soccer, summer matches, and camp"; he also coached younger players in our Community Center program. He writes, "I did the deal! I'm prepared. Bring it on." His preparation deserves a "well done" from me followed by a discussion of his off-season training and plans for college.

Other discussion points and questions that I might pose as a result of reading Jonathan's Preseason Thoughts include the following:

- "Tell me about the issues you faced as a Community Center soccer coach of elementary school kids."
- "What did you do to work on your 'squirrely' left foot?"
- "You have demanding courses this year in school—how will you keep up with school work and soccer?"
- "In your opinion, in what ways does 'playing up' against better teams help you and your teammates?"

These kinds of questions and the ensuing discussions push athletes to think and speak like coaches. In terms of heightened learning, such talk helps move athletes toward that elusive next level.

Preseason Thoughts provides the coaching staff with another level of insight about new athletes. Through a lens beyond the field of play—or the court, pitch, pool, range, beach, course, mountain, arena, team room, mat, or classroom—we come to know first-year and transfer players. We have an opportunity to hear about the new players' dedication, self-perception, sports mind, and academics. It's important to realize that writing from some new players may either be embellished or not reveal the full story of their athletic backgrounds.

For many newcomers, receiving a Team Notebook from a captain or coach often proves to be a unique experience and tends to elevate the stature of the team in the new player's eyes. Granted, many coaches use playbooks or handbooks that will include a schedule and team rules, but a Team Notebook extends the potential of traditional playbooks and handbooks by inviting athletes to contribute their thinking through writing.

Coaches may deliberate whether they want their assistant coaches and/or trainers to read Team Notebook entries. Some coaches believe that this common experience adds to the staff's conversations about individual athletes and the team in general. Furthermore, used as references, the Team Notebook sheets will offer points of contact with athletes for future discussions about training and competition, college and work. Some coaches believe that Team Notebook entries are private writing to be shared with just the head coach. As always, your job is to decide what approach serves your athletes, your team, and you most effectively.

When Athletes Write

When athletes write about their preparation for the competitive season, several benefits emerge. For dedicated athletes, those who have fully involved themselves in off-season training and arrive at preseason fit and determined, writing Preseason Thoughts can build confidence. In addition, sharing their accomplishments with coaches, training staff, and perhaps with teammates proves motivational. All of us appreciate being recognized for our efforts.

For those athletes who have only marginally prepared for the competitive season, responding to Preseason Thoughts can be a hollow experience. However, the act of writing may also serve as a reality check of "what I did not do to prepare" and this writing may impact long-term player development by serving as an incentive. Writing about poor preparation won't necessarily inspire an athlete to train to new levels in the future, but then again it might. At the very least, this writing activity can help athletes see the emerging picture of their athletic identity and serve as one more piece of a larger wake-up call. To me, it has always been profoundly curious (and wildly irritating) how some athletes don't recognize the connection of off-season preparation to in-season performance. Team Notebook pages, both preseason and postseason entries, may help those athletes more quickly realize the relationship of off-season practice to performance.

When Coaches Read

With a team of twenty-two athletes, it might take me 20–30 minutes to read a collection of Preseason Thoughts. As I highlight selected passages on my set of photocopies, I am delighted to discover new details about players I may have known for years (e.g., they lift weights every other day with their dad or jog each day with their sister). When I read the pages from travel team athletes that I don't know, I tend to spend more time reading and highlighting selected passages. There are several variables—number of players, length of writing, and penmanship!—but quite honestly, reading Team Notebook pages is rarely, if ever, a chore.

I'm intrigued at how athletes view past performances. I'd like to say I've found some pattern to their written responses, but I haven't. Initially, I thought that my most veteran players would write the most balanced analyses of their previous season's play, and that more novice players wouldn't be able to find all of the words to describe their strengths and challenges. But that's not always the case.

I am not surprised by how my view of the previous season is restated by so many of my veteran players. In some cases it's as if players are transcribing my post-season banquet talk in their reflections. Reading such entries reminds me of the influence coaches have. In other cases, my athletes' writing teaches me about what they need and what might benefit the team.

When you read through your athletes' responses, you will hear about an athlete's training and competition, but don't be surprised if there are comments about school, work, or family. If a player shares that a parent has lost a job or a sibling is ill, this knowledge has the potential to help you and your staff work more thoughtfully with the athlete.

As we read our athletes' writing, we must remember the position we have placed them in. Our athletes know that the main audience for their writing is us, their coaches. This reality creates an interesting dynamic. Sometimes you will read glowing passages that athletes know we would like to hear. We will also read entries that are difficult to address. When reading athletes' writing, we have to allow their thinking. In the end, the pages of a Team Notebook belong to the athlete-authors, and the ultimate purpose of the writing is to help them learn by exploring ideas and to make sense of their time as an athlete.

Individual Sports

For athletes in more individualized sports like track, tennis, or Nordic skiing, written reflections like Pre- or Postseason Thoughts can have a different look. One prime example comes from long-time Nordic coach Pete Phillips of Burke Mountain Academy in East Burke, Vermont. After we discussed writing to learn in athletics, Pete tapped into his experiences and materials from various coaching professionals to develop two written analyses for his athletes, Demand Analysis and Capacity Analysis (Figures 2.4 and 2.5).

Pete explained that he was "asking the athlete to think about the demands of the sport, and then to further consider one's own capacities to meet [those] demands and further still to use those thoughts to give shape to goals. . . ." As a coach, Pete has always found that the cornerstone of his coaching involved "the idea of athlete thought and feedback" (personal correspondence, December 1, 2010).

BURKE MOUNTAIN ACADEMY

PASSION FOR SKIING. LEARNING FOR LIFE.

Capacity Analysis

Athlete: Thomas Rabon

Physical Analysis

Aerobic Endurance: *I have a good amount of aerobic endurance. I'm able to push my body for an extended period of time at high RPMs. I feel like I have a good base of endurance for this year.*

Strength: *Strength is something that I've worked on quite a lot this fall, and so I have a good amount of it. I have a lot to use, but I need to use more of it.*

Flexibility: *I have a low range of flexibility where I should have more. I need to work on being more flexible because if I do this then I will in turn be able to use more of my strength that is just sitting there. I need to be more mobile and flexible to extend farther out over my skis.*

Explosiveness: *I think I am fairly explosive. I definitely could do more work with it though.* Spenst hop *is something that I do fairly well, but I think I could do more and get better.*

Speed: *On an average day I can be fairly speedy. As a rule though, I haven't been the best sprinter while skiing. Running I can be fast, but I need to find how to transfer that onto the skis.*

Coordination: *I need to spend more time looking at video of myself against better skiers. If I do this and then sleep on it/go work out afterwards I feel that I'll be able to have an image in my head and get my timing a little bit better than it is right now. My arms need to slow their tempo down so that I can ski bigger and get farther over my skis so that I can crunch more. In the skate race I think I was doing this a lot better than I had been in the past. It's coming along I think.*

Technique: *Kind of the same as coordination; I need to get my timing a little better/get my hips forward more/extend my arms down the trail and not up/crunch more. All of this will make my skiing more efficient and therefore faster.*

Tactics: *I think that I'm a good tactical skier in the longer distance races. In sprints I feel like I tend to get a little jittery and just fall in behind people. I need to learn how to make quick decisions about passing or letting up at a certain point to become a better sprinter.*

Physiological Capacity: *My ability to deal with pain is high. I don't have a hard time staying at race pace for an extended period of time when I am prepared for it. As we've talked*

Figure 2.4 Capacity Analysis (Nordic Skiing) (*continued*) *about, I need to get my head wrapped around the race part better though. I get caught up in results and this affects my skiing in the wrong ways sometimes.*

Social Skills: *My social skills with the team are pretty good. I feel like I get along with most everyone. Obviously there are people that I can become annoyed with, but I do my best to overlook it. I think I do a good job of keeping the joking around to time when we are not working out, but I think that as the race season approaches it will be a good idea to tone it down a bit and try to be seen as more of a team leader. I'll be on time and prepared with what I need to do.*

Goals

Results Goals: *I want solid performances at Nationals in Rumford in early January. Matt tells me that I better be going for the Scandinavian Team and I will, but I won't be upset if I don't make the team. That could be more of a realistic goal for next year, given that I stay healthy. I am hopeful to make the Junior Nationals team for New England, and with that comes good, consistent performances at the Eastern Cups and Super Tour.*

Performance Goals: *I want to be a bigger skier by the middle of the year. I plan on working on extending my arms down the trail, and skiing loosely (esp. classic). I want to crunch more while I am skiing both techniques of course. Also I want to work on tempo and explosiveness as well as balance, because all of these together will make me a more efficient skier/faster skier.*

Process Goals: *At times where I have the opportunity to stretch I will take the time to do so. I have a limited range of movement in my upper body especially, and I'll be more powerful if I can use the muscle up there. On training skis I will balance on one ski as I go down a hill with my hips forward for as long as I can so that I become balanced and can glide more while V2ing and V2 alternating. I will do this on both legs equally so that I am not going to favor one side. I will also V1 on each side equally when we are doing training skis so that energy can be evenly used when I am tired in a race. I will swing my arms more than necessary in both skate and classic techniques to get myself used to staying loose and throwing myself down the trail.*

If I take my Goals to heart and really try to put into action my process goals I feel like I have a good season ahead of me. I, along with my parents, have put too much on the line for me to come to this school and learn to my fullest potential for me not to try my hardest. I am willing to take a huge risk to achieve the mental and physical goals that I have set for myself this year and for the years to come, and I have a large stake in the sport as a result of that. I am willing to put in my full effort to reach my potential. For the next training block I'll be focused on preparing for Nationals by immersing myself in my process goals as well as staying healthy and stress free. That means getting my work done on time and getting enough sleep at night. One thing to look forward to is having Evan come to my place in Maine right after Christmas so we can ski Rumford a bunch before the crowds arrive. He's a good person to train with because we both can have fun when we're not training, but when it comes time to go to work outs we are really focused on our goals.

Figure 2.4 *(continued)*

Demand Analysis

Athlete: Thomas Rabon

Physical Demands

Aerobic Endurance:
The ability to sustain a high heart rate through an entire race and go hard the whole way.
Core strength/endurance
Flexibility
Explosiveness for power while pushing off a ski or poling hard.
Speed

Coordination: *Timing with arms and legs needs to be correct because power is lost if not. Also balance is key with coordination.*

Technique: *A skier needs to have fluid, efficient technique. They need to be forward moving and using their muscle mass to the best of their ability.*

Tactics: *Warm up and cool down routines. The ability to inspect a course and from there know where you want to go as hard as possible/not waste energy/ make a move in a mass start race.*

Psychological Capacity: *The ability to know that you're in a lot of pain and push through it, or that you had a bad race and get back out there with your head up for the next one.*

Social Skills: *While racing be able to have no problem yelling track or something; but on the same team working well with everyone so that we can all train effectively. Cooperation with others is very important. At the same time the ability to have the skill to go off on your own and do your own workout without others influencing you socially is needed as well.*

Figure 2.5 Demand Analysis (Nordic Skiing)

After Coach Phillips instituted the written reflections with his Burke skiers, he explained that the analyses were "initiated primarily to help athletes put a more careful lens on their participation in a very difficult sport; to help them be realistic in goal setting and to help provide them with a sort of chart." Asked what he thought about the results, he wrote,

> [T]his particular exercise is producing valuable material for us as coaches at a level far beyond my expectations. The athletes have given these [analyses] some thought and have come up with surprisingly candid and perspicacious observations. There are many things I have already taken away and am working on integrating into individual training programs.

Pete also highlighted how the reflections helped his athletes create result-oriented goals and recognize "that there are concrete steps one can take . . . toward a result goal. There is a chart that gets [an athlete] closer and better prepared for the showdown [of the race]" (2010).

Activities to Use with Preseason Thoughts

You may decide that writing Preseason Thoughts is enough for your athletes and follow-up activities aren't necessary. No matter what, however, your athletes will have impromptu conversations about the notebook pages. Our athletes talk about such things in the weight room, while commuting back and forth to practice, and on social network sites like Facebook. They may also quiz you about the pages during stretching or classroom sessions. In addition, assistant coaches and other team personnel, if they serve as notebook readers, also discuss the athletes' responses both formally and informally. Those various conversations extend the learning value of the notebooks. However, if you want to add more to the experience, there are activities you may use to complement your athletes' writing.

The following exercises provide a variety of ways to extend your athletes' thinking and thereby broaden their learning. Select an activity or two that fits your program, and there's a good chance that it will prompt the kinds of discussions that will benefit your athletes, team, and program.

A Synthesis

A synthesis of selected quotations taken from your athletes' Team Notebook pages will help you and your athletes see the range of thinking among teammates. There are more than several ways to use the synthesis effectively; for example, try this one:

You or an assistant could select athletes' comments from each section of Preseason Thoughts. Perhaps a manager could type them out. If you have a large team, select representative quotations as I have in Figure 2.6. Even though the athletes' quotations are usually short and

Preseason Thoughts: What We Said (abbreviated version)

Player Preparation for this Season

Playing with a men's league team.

Distance running, going to high school tryouts, weight training

Summer soccer (summer league & Bay State Games), running, push-ups

New attitude, I know why/what I'm playing for. In best shape I have been in during past 5 years.

I ran 2–3 times a week and occasionally would play small sided games with friends.

I played on two teams, went to the gym 3 days a week. Did my former high school's 2-week double sessions before coming here. Ran every day 3 miles (except Sundays).

Jogging almost every day for almost five miles. Last 30 seconds of 4.3 miles—sprinted—push-ups, sit-ups. Eating healthy & stretching.

Lifting 2–4 times a week. Running every other day 3–5 miles around lake and back to my house.

Ran the bay every other day in the last 3 weeks. Did push ups & sit-ups every night. Played soccer every night.

Shooting, running long distance, juggling.

Running two miles every day. Eat healthy and eat at the right time.

Lifting 2–4 times a week. Playing 2–3 times a week. Running 2–3 times a week.

I have lost 33 pounds since I last played. I played summer soccer & ran as much as I could despite my injury.

Running usually 2–3 miles every other day. Some plyometrics. Push-ups and sit-ups.

I ran as much as I could but missed many days because of work.

Kick around a few times a week. Ran twice a week 2 miles.

Played Super-Y and adult league this summer. Did stationary bike daily for at least a half hour. Sit-ups every day and ball workout 3 days a week.

Played soccer in the New Haven Boulevard League.

Figure 2.6 Preseason Thoughts Synthesis (abbreviated version) (*continued*)

Team Strengths Last Season

We were close and had a common goal.

Resiliency. We bounced back extremely well after an extremely slow start. Good coaching. Good listeners. Hard workers.

Many seniors and skilled freshmen. Two good keepers. Fitness was good. Smooth passing throughout the team.

Team chemistry.

Teamwork, attitude, coaching staff, leadership, defensive.

Solid defense, solid goalie, respect for each other.

We came back from a terrible season & had our best season in 15 years or so.

Finishing, possession of the ball, defending as a team.

Communication, ability to improve

Fitness, team morale, determination, perseverance

We all had respect for one another.

We had a very good defense.

Team Weaknesses Last Season

Playing SIMPLE! Utilizing our flanks. Finishing. Playing hard for 90 minutes.

Didn't know how to achieve goal.

Youth. We had a lot of really young kids. Bad start to the season.

Size, finishing, poor health (pulled muscles etc . . .)

Midfield, depth, scoring goals, discipline, defending and offending free kicks.

Scoring and possessions. We couldn't possess the ball as well as we should have.

Fitness injury.

Poor attitudes & lack of team unity.

Lack of focus for 90 minutes. Difficulty scoring, finishing.

Weak outside players. Goalie (enough said).

Played really bad when going down. Needed to win the BIG game.

Failure in final third [offensive third of the field]

Focus during training sessions.

Figure 2.6 *(continued)*

interesting, don't overwhelm your team with too many pages. In Figure 2.6, I am only including lists of athletes' quotations from three of the seven Preseason Thoughts prompts.

Ask the athletes to read the collection and to circle teammates' quotations that they find interesting and might like to discuss. As an introduction to conducting team discussions, you may wish to organize a *reading-in-the-round*: have the players sit in a circle and ask them to read aloud one of the quotations they selected. Go from athlete to athlete without stopping. Hearing the collection will reveal areas of interest. Then, move on to either full-team or small-group discussions:

- *Full-Team Discussion*: Discuss the quotations of interest in a full-team setting. Coaches or talented senior players will guide the discussion by posing questions or making observations about specific quotations like this example on "Team Unity":
  - I noticed a number of players wrote that last year we had strong team unity. What made this possible?
  - In what ways could we build the same level of team unity this year?
  - What actions or comments by athletes weaken team unity?

  It may be a good idea to write these questions and observations in advance of the full team discussion.

  Depending on the age and maturity level of your athletes, you may wish to set discussion boundaries in advance (e.g., do not criticize a teammate's quotation or comment). Use guiding questions such as "What can we learn about last year's team from this quotation?" or "How many of you felt the same as this player about last year's team and our strengths?" You may also want to suggest a time limit and make a point of setting the time on your watch.

  It's important to keep these discussions productive and to avoid excess griping. It's also vital to show respect for each athlete's opinion. For example, if an athlete says something like "I think this sentence is pointless," ask the athlete to elaborate: "That comment doesn't help the team. Tell us more. Under what circumstances might such a quotation be useful?"

Ultimately, the point of such exercises is to unpack thinking and discover team strengths, challenges, and understandings. You'll also notice that, in time, athletes will begin to use more specific language when writing and talking about team and individual performances. When team talk does elevate, you'll know learning is happening.

- *Small-Group Discussions*: Divide the team into discussion groups of four to six athletes. You may divide the groups in any number of ways, including

  offense/defense,
  grade level or class,
  interest of athletes, or
  mixed groups (starters, first in, 2nd team; blondes, brown hair . . .).

  Assign each small group a certain topic area such as offense, scoring, off-season training, or personal goals. Have them highlight quotations that fit under those areas. You may also divide the groups by the various sections of Preseason Thoughts.

  Provide each group with a sheet of 2′ × 3′ chart paper and a large-print marker to list their top three discussion points. Give the groups specific instructions with respect to the amount of time they have to discuss and how long they will share with the whole team (2–3 minutes). Finally, remind your athletes of the purpose of the exercise: We want to learn more and to improve our play.

  After 10–15 minutes of small-group discussion, have each group report their thinking to the whole team. As coach, you may need to guide the discussions, depending on your athletes' maturity and knowledge of the sport.

One-on-One Discussions: Coach and Athlete

Preseason Thoughts create a platform for coaches to have more informed discussions with athletes. Guided by the athlete's own words, a coach may discuss an athlete's preparation, instructional needs, academics (if appropriate), and outlook on the upcoming season. One word of caution: If you want your athletes to write honestly and fully, don't criticize the athlete's writing. Try to focus on the positives by bringing out the athlete's ideas. Time: 5–10 minutes.

Quantifying Preseason Training

Using a page in the Notes Section of the Team Notebook, ask your athletes to add up their training hours and include the activities (e.g., playing the sport, weight training, running) in preparation for the upcoming season. If they don't keep a training log, they will have to estimate the time to the best of their abilities. Then ask them to figure out if this level of training is sufficient; if not, ask them to devise a new training program. Such an activity will help many athletes see the strength or weakness of their training. Time: 5–10 minutes.

Comparing One Preseason to Another

Using a page in the Notes Section of the Team Notebook, your athletes will compare their off-season training for the previous 2-years by making lists of athletic activities. Naturally, they will have to rely on their memories unless you ask them to keep a training log of off-season activities. Afterward, ask questions such as

- Did your hours of training increase from one preseason to the next?
- Did you train more sport-specific in one preseason as compared to the other?
- Now that you've looked at your previous two off-seasons, design the next one.

What changes do you propose? Time: 5–10 minutes.

Last Season

Using a page in the Notes Section of the Team Notebook, your athletes will sketch what they feel was the most effective alignment of players for the previous season and explain their decision in writing. Time: 3–5 minutes.

Best Moment of Last Season

Using a page in the Notes Section of the Team Notebook, your athletes will describe and sketch, if appropriate, the best moment of the previous season. That moment could come from a competition, a training session, a bus trip, or any team gathering. Time: 5 minutes.

Imagining the Best Moment of This Season

Using a page in the Notes Section of the Team Notebook, your athletes will create a "best moment" for the upcoming season. This kind of writing has the quality of sport psychology's mental imagery and elicits the same benefits. Time: 5 minutes.

Feedback from a "Thinking Partner"

Have your athletes share their Preseason Thoughts with a teammate. You might put names in a hat so players are divided randomly. An alternative thinking partner: Ask your players to discuss their preseason writing with a parent/guardian, an adult, a former player, or an athlete or coach from different sport. Instead of a discussion, you could ask your players to have their Thinking Partner write their observations in a letter that will be included in the Notes Section. Time: 30 minutes.

Songs of Last Season

For a near-total break in the action, perhaps at a preseason gathering, have your athletes write a song that recounts the previous season. Use familiar songs like "The Beverly Hillbillies," "Camp Granada," or "Gilligan's Island," and divide your athletes in small groups by class, position on the team, or their own choice of groupings. New team members and first-year students can easily join in. The end results will be funny and at times irreverent; however, the depth of thinking that goes into this writing activity will compel athletes to talk broadly about the previous season. Collect the lyrics and photocopy for the Notes Section of Team Notebooks. You might think such an activity is just for youngsters—not so! Those of us who coach college-aged athletes have heard more than our fair share of songs on long trips. Time: 30 minutes.

Team Sociogram

A sociogram gives a coach an opportunity to see where players fall within a team's social ladder. Who among your players is liked, trusted, or admired . . . and who's not. Here are a few questions that could serve this purpose:

- What three players on our team would you like to compete with at the next level?
- Which three players would you want to coach your younger brother or sister?
- If you had an important examination coming up, which three players on our team would you most want to study with?
- Which of your teammates would your favorite grandparent, uncle, or aunt enjoy and why?
- Which three players on our team would you enjoy traveling with?

Ask your players to briefly explain their selections. The purpose? Once you collect the athletes' writing, you'll see who on the team is regarded and who goes unmentioned. This information could help explain certain team issues. What could you do with such writing? Create a synthesis, share certain lines with certain players, and read the collection of reasons without giving names. You might also ask questions during mid- or late-season as a way to identify who, in your players' eyes, would make a good captain for the coming year. You might conduct a sociogram at any point during the season to raise your players' awareness about how they influence one another. Just creating the list can make players think about their roles on your team and benefit both the players and the coach. Time: 5–10 minutes

And so . . .

Beginning your sports season with Preseason Thoughts adds a new dimension to your coaching practice, to your team as a unit, and to individual athletes. This section of the Team Notebook sets a studious tone while helping athletes and coaches think about past and future performances. Such reflection provides opportunities for wide-ranging discussions, deeper reflection, and a big-time reality check. We all know that new sports seasons are full of promise, yet tinged with anxiety. Writing can help.

Chapter Three

Competition Analysis I: Telling the Story of Your Game

My high school players have circled at the center of the pitch after a night soccer match. The boys have completed their team stretches and now each takes care of his individual needs: shedding tape, stretching more, and wolfing snacks. . . . One after another the players finish their routines and reach into their soccer kits for their Team Notebooks and open them to a Match Analysis I. I watch silently from outside the circle near our bench. Two of the captains, Jeff and Ryan, debrief the match with one another while the rest of the players press pen to paper.

On the touchline behind me a pack of middle school players gaze at the varsity team. It's easy to read the younger boys' minds as they jostle one another, eyes transfixed on the circle of older players. Over at our opponents' bench, players speak with parents and each other; some sulk off to the side. Occasionally, the visitors dressed in scarlet and white glance toward our post-match classroom.

I watch as their coach finishes an interview with our local sports reporter and wonder how the coach will unpack the 3-1 loss with his team. And how about his boys? Furtive glances from a few suggest that perhaps they'd like to be circled up making sense of what happened in the match. What will happen next for these athletes? Will they climb onto their bus and rant about the loss, complain about the officiating, or whisper about their central defender's inability to stop our all-state striker Danny? Will their coach demand silence for the ninety-minute bus ride home through the moonlit mountains of western Maine? Does silent suffering help us learn? Coaching can be so complicated.

Our posse of parents and caregivers wait patiently for their sons—they know our post-match routine. So does the collection of girlfriends and high school buddies. It's what we do, win, lose, or draw after every match.

Most players complete the Match Analysis prompts in 2–3 minutes. With a hug from dad or a quick kiss from that special someone, the kids melt into the darkness with their cobalt blue Adidas kits slung over their shoulders and the hip-loose swagger that victory provides. Some players ask to take the analysis page home to think about, while one or two stare blankly into the night sky, replaying the match, a missed opportunity, or their long night on the bench.

That mid-September evening, now nearly 20 years ago, is permanently fixed in my mind. I witnessed my players' seamless connection to the match through their writing. I knew after reading their entries later that night that they had been pushed to think and then write about the game, and that the act of writing clarified my brief post-game talk and our team discussion. I also realized from experience that our talk and their writing shaped the boys' discussions with teammates, friends, family, my assistant, and me. All of this, I'm convinced, creates a condition for players to live more fully as students of the game. This mindset creates a fairly balanced, impartial view of the final outcome. Getting them there—where they view the match as participant (involved) and spectator (observer)—is part of my job as a coach. The Match Analysis is one way to move them toward this balanced stance.

Organizing

The majority of my athletes complete the Match Analysis right after the competition. An assistant coach, captain, manager, or I collect the notebook sheets for photocopying. My goal was to hand back the original sheets to the players at the very next practice. I required my high school players to bring their team kits to every practice; those bags included equipment such as running shoes, soccer studs, shin guards, water bottles, practice jerseys, and Team Notebooks with a pen.

A Closer Look

The prompts on a Competition Analysis I help athletes reflect on their individual performances as well as those of their teammates and opponents. Naturally, you can revise any aspect of this sheet as well as the title to fit your particular sport (e.g., Game, Meet, or Race Analysis). These prompts tend to steer players away from reducing a game result to one-dimensional accounts like "the referees had it in for us." The analysis helps players gain perspective and, in large and small ways, moves them toward thinking as coaches and—always—students of the game.

In Figure 3.1, you'll see Jonathan's analysis as sweeper, soccer's last-line defender before the goalkeeper. This match was our 4th countable league match of the season and came after a four-match preseason including an all-day tournament. In addition, during our preseason we enjoyed hosting a secondary school soccer team from near London, England, for ten days. St. Clement Danes School in Chorleywood played well beyond our level; that challenge improved our play immensely.

Unpacking Jonathan's Writing

Reading players' responses takes practice. When I first started using notebooks, I rode the wave of my players' comments, including those responses that seemed like criticisms, indifference, *and* compliments. I learned almost immediately to allow the players to be in charge of their notebook pages, not to hover, and to avoid commenting on or being moved one way or the other by individual entries. In fact, rarely did I speak with a player about a specific entry or write a response. My main approach with the Competition Analysis I was to read the collection after a match and then, at the next practice session, to speak in general

Match Analysis I

Player: Jonathan

Falcons v. Leavitt Date: 9/17 Place: Away Final: 1-0 Win

Records: Falcons: 4 . . . W 0 . . . L 0 . . . D Opponent: 3 . . . W 1 . . . L 0 . . . D

- *My strengths as a player in today's match:* Maintained defense's compactness. Right amount of talk—I didn't talk too much like at Lisbon. I had a brilliant run through the midfield into the attacking third . . . ☺

- *My weaknesses as a player in today's match:* I could have been more supportive of Jason. When I encourage him he plays better.

- *Team strengths in today's match:* We worked as a team—great support—positive comments . . . Good halftime adjustments.

- *Team weaknesses in today's match:* We could have been more inventive in attack during the 2nd half. We used Matt too much.

- *Opponent's strengths:* They never let down. #9 had warp-speed. His runs opened space and chances on goal.

- *Opponent's weaknesses:* Their midfielders and forwards did not mark us well in attack.

- *What was the "difference" in today's match:* Our midfielders support of the forwards . . . and, did I mention, a brilliant run by the sweeper?

- *What team adjustment would you suggest for the next match against this opponent:* #9=FAST. Move Dusty? More variety in attack.

- *Other comments about team strategy, attitude, preparation. . . .*
  We were prepared! The seniors had us ready to play. Un-DE-feated!

Figure 3.1 Competition Analysis I (Soccer)

terms about the collection of writing. Even then, that did not happen after each match. Many times addressing their Team Notebooks wasn't as important as getting out on the field and practicing.

I do my best to stay as balanced as possible as a reader. It's curious that knowing your athletes well can be both a gift and a complexity when reading their notebook entries. Sometimes a player's writing is probing or experimental, and these ideas may not fit with your vision of a particular player. Again, let players have their own space with respect to their Team Notebook responses. If you want honest, gut-level writing and as a result deeper thinking, just let them write.

I've taken the following lines of writing from Jonathan's Match Analysis I page. Let me give a brief picture of my thinking in his response to his thoughts:

> *My strengths as a player in today's match:* Maintained defense's compactness. Right amount of talk—I didn't talk too much like at Lisbon. I had a brilliant run through the midfield into the attacking third . . . ☺

As the principal defender, Jonathan understands his responsibility in maintaining order and compactness (i.e., a tight, organized formation) in the back third of the team's alignment. Since we had worked tirelessly on maintaining our shape during summer league, at soccer camp, and throughout our preseason, organization tops Jonathan's response.

The young man's writing about communication ("Right amount of talk—I didn't talk too much like at Lisbon") shows that he has applied his learning from one match to another. In the previous match against Lisbon, Jonathan gave too many directions to his three defensive mates. My comment to him after Lisbon focused on his talk, and his post-match comments reassured me that "he got the message." Finally, throughout the summer and preseason we joked about defensive players creating those one or two brilliant runs per match that surprise the opponent and open up the field for an attack with numbers. In this instance, I had hollered "Brilliant run!" to Jonathan after his diagonal run through the attacking third just to the top of the penalty area.

> *My weaknesses as a player in today's match:* I could have been more supportive of Jason. When I encourage him he plays better.

With this entry, Jonathan reveals his understanding of the difference he can make in the play of a less confident teammate. When reading such a response, I see that the player understands his larger role within the game. This writing is a sure sign of a player's ability to lead.

> *Team strengths in today's match:* We worked as a team—great support—positive comments . . . Good halftime adjustments.

Jonathan's comments ("We worked as a team—great support—positive comments . . .") paralleled what I emphasized in both my halftime talk and post-match debriefing. To varying degrees athletes do hear a coach's words, so it's not uncommon to find such retelling in players' notebook writing. In addition, since soccer is a fairly straightforward game, a team's strengths and weaknesses are often easily identifiable. Jonathan's final line ("Good halftime adjustments") referred to two changes I made in defensive assignments.

I am not concerned if players echo my comments in their writing. Some players may not trust their own observations of the game while others fret about being "wrong." It doesn't take long at all for most players to gain confidence. In some instances their words are not retellings of my halftime or post-game observations; sometimes their words simply tell the story of the game as they saw it. However, if your athletes continually serve your game observations back to you, I suggest delaying your post-game debrief on occasion and have the athletes write first.

> *Team weaknesses in today's match:* We could have been more inventive in attack during the 2nd half. We used Matt too much.

Jonathan's observation of our lack of inventiveness in attack raised my awareness. I knew we used Matthew a great deal. An all-conference player with speed and creativity, Matthew tends to demand the ball and when he receives it, something positive happens. Jonathan's wording—"We could have been more inventive in attack"—raises issues such as how opponents prepare for us (e.g., "Matthew is their main weapon"), how balanced our attack is, and how surprising we are as a team. Jonathan's words led me to discuss our offense more comprehensively with my assistant and then the team.

A somewhat similar experience happened to a college coaching friend of mine who uses Team Notebooks. While reading Match Analysis I entries from the third match of the season, Coach Mike Keller of the University of Southern Maine Huskies discovered that more than several of his younger players were confused about their roles in the 3-5-2 team formation (3 defenders, 5 midfielders, and 2 strikers). Some players felt the team would be more productive with a 4-4-2. Through team discussions, more explicit coaching, and an unsuccessful trial run of the 4-4-2, the Huskies learned the 3-5-2 and became more confident with the system. Certainly, Coach Keller would have recognized the issue with the 3-5-2; however, this veteran coach believes his players' written comments brought the matter to his attention more quickly.

> *Opponent's strengths:* They never let down. #9 had warp-speed. His runs opened space and chances on goal.
>
> *Opponent's weaknesses:* Their midfielders and forwards did not mark us well in attack.

These observations of our opponents' strengths and weaknesses show Jonathan's balance as participant-observer. To be sure, their #9 had boundless energy and his speedy runs off the ball often had more than one of our players chasing him. His speed and movement opened up space for his team to create more passing and deeper penetration toward and into the attacking third.

As Jonathan notes, our opponents' midfielders and forwards did not mark as tightly or as intensely as they should have. After we won the ball and moved toward their goal, we'd have decent space for passing because of our opponent's lethargic defending.

> *What was the "difference" in today's match:* Our midfielders support of the forwards . . . did I mention a brilliant run by the sweeper?

Jonathan recognized how well our forwards and midfielders worked together in the match. They attacked with numbers and supported one another fully. Though he didn't mention this strength, our midfielders' and forwards' communication with one another allowed their good work. Finally, Jonathan's light-hearted personality surfaced after this win when he again mentions his confident run from the defense through the attacking third.

> *What team adjustment would you suggest for the next match against this opponent:* #9=FAST. Move Dusty? More variety in attack.

Jonathan's response reinforces his earlier comments about our opponents. His adjustment suggestions mirror the changes we made at the half—and indeed, if all things remain constant, we'll use the same approach in the next match.

> *Other comments about team strategy, attitude, preparation. . . .* We were prepared! The seniors had us ready to play. Un-DE-feated!

As a field leader on our team at a key defensive position, Jonathan compliments our senior leaders and celebrates our undefeated run so far in the season. I find this kind of unselfishness inspiring and indicative of a team captain.

Activities to Use with the Competition Analysis I

Again, you may decide that your athletes don't need additional activities to complement their writing in the Team Notebook. However, whether to extend a conversation, add variety to learning activities, or focus on a particular aspect of a game or practice session, follow-up activities using your players' writing have the potential to help them become more effective communicators and to promote learning (Parker and Goodkin, 1987 as cited in http://wac.colostate.edu/intro/pop4a.cfm). The following activities may prove beneficial for your team or for individual athletes:

A Synthesis

There exist many different approaches to creating a synthesis from your players' notebooks. The lists can be used for small and large group discussion starters. As a coach you can also use a synthesis to create more writing activities for your players and, if appropriate, for your staff. For example, you could pass out the collection and ask your players and staff to read and then write for 3 minutes in reaction to the synthesis.

"What We Said," the synthesis from *Preseason Thoughts,* captured a variety of thinking from the players. One shorter version of a synthesis utilizes quotations from one or two of the prompts. For example, using the Match Analysis I Team Strengths and Weaknesses the team could give a glimpse of all players' thinking. Look at the quotations from the men's team at the University of Southern Maine in Figure 3.2. As you'll read, the Huskies enjoyed a comeback win in this match. Do you think the list of Team Weaknesses highlights some of the reason(s) the Huskies went behind in the match? This question and others make for interesting conversations and follow-up activities. Indeed, there are several different ways of unpacking such collections. Here is an activity that works with the Competition Analysis I Strengths and Weaknesses synthesis:

1. Ask players to read the synthesis and then take 3 minutes to write on a page in their Notes Section what they noticed as common themes or issues in the collection.
2. Divide the players into groups according to position, year in school/age, or their choice. Ask players to discuss what they noticed and to select a spokesperson from the group to present one, two, or three observations.
3. After all groups have presented, ask if anyone has a question, comment, or observation. You may end the team activity with the athletes' comments or your own. I often limit my input during notebook discussion times to build confidence among players and encourage them to think more like coaches.

Note to an Opponent

The day after a game, give your players 3–5 minutes to write a note to an opponent—usually, they'll write to the primary person they defended. If your sport is like baseball or track, ask the players to pick an opponent who performed exceptionally well or who struggled. Your players could highlight an opponent's strengths or weaknesses. In the

What We Said about the Comeback Win

Team Strengths	*Team Weaknesses*
Came back AGAIN	Got down and didn't hustle
Coming back together as a team to win	Not talking—playing down to their level
Did not give up, scoring goals	Was not consistent throughout the game at passing—did not come out like we used to
Didn't give up	defense, sloppy ball passing—more passing
Didn't give up	wasn't playing well
Came back from goal down	ball watching
Come back win Good set pieces	Midfield recovery
Heart, battled back	Not *focused!!*
Didn't give up	played down to their level
Came from behind to win	Didn't press much, didn't play as a team
ability to come back, effort	lack of concentration too much 1 v. 1
Came back, won when we played bad	Slow, outplayed in midfield for most of the game
Never gave up *COME BACK TEAM*	Shitty first-half defense Came in thinking it was easy
Come back	Came out weak, sloppy, unprepared
Kept attacking	Came out flat
Persistence, heart, will	1st ten minutes 2nd half
Moved the ball well, never gave up, and able to finish	lack of communication at times
Resilience	Didn't play our game
Ability to rally back	Mental preparation—concentration no hunger on defense

Figure 3.2 Synthesis of Quotations from USM Players

case of an opponent's weakness, a player should offer advice. Here's an example from a high school soccer match:

> Dear # 3 Right Back,
>
> We played against each other on Thursday night and you could not stop me. Every time I attacked with the ball down the left touchline you lunged at the ball—you ALWAYS tried to take the ball away from me and never really just tried to delay my attack. My coach tells us that there are four D's in defending—
>
> - Deny the opponent the ball
> - Delay the opponent when he has the ball
> - Destroy . . . win the ball!
> - Develop an attack once you have ball
>
> You should practice shadowing an attacking offender, pushing him to the touchline so he can't get a full look at the goal. Delaying stops him from advancing toward the goal and gets other players behind the ball to defend. When the player miskicks the ball or plays it too far ahead, you win the ball. I'm glad I'm not really giving you this letter because I like playing against you! I scored and got two assists. HA! See you in a few weeks, sucka.
>
> Your nightmare,
>
> Chad
>
> Sailors #9

After your players write these notes, you can create small groups to have them share their writing. There's bound to be laughter (especially after a win), but also count on discussions that underscore team, individual tactics, and game highlights. These notes may also be used as the genesis of conversations between a coach and an athlete or a coach and an offensive or defensive unit. Obviously, these notes won't be mailed to the athletes from the opposing team; however, saving this writing in the Notes Section will allow players to refer to their thinking if there's a second game with the opponent.

Please Note: Such a learning activity can be invaluable for an athlete. Chad's response above is both smart and playful, but don't be surprised if you receive cheeky notes that have minimal learning value and merely showcase a player's troublesome side. As with all team activities, put a stop to this behavior immediately with a one-to-one discussion or a quick note back to the athlete: "I know you're trying to be funny, but now, in your second attempt, I'd like to see a more serious note."

Note to Opponent's Coach

This note might highlight the strengths or weaknesses of a team. Your athletes may write suggestions to the opposing coach or focus on ways the visiting team exploited your own.

> Dear Coach,
>
> You have a great team. They are disciplined and organized and the kids were good guys even though they kicked our butts! Your players had wicked good talk. They supported each other with talk. Our coach always tells us to play the way we are facing. At tonight's match I could see that. I was impressed how your midfielders used their defenders so well. They got out of a lot of trouble with quick back passes. I also thought your one and two touch passes were *useful* as our coach says. We learned a lot today and I am proud of the way we played even though we lost 3–1. Some day I hope our team will play like yours. Good luck with the rest of your season.
>
> Sincerely,
>
> Kevin

Such positive writing shared with other players can lead to terrific discussions. Clearly, knowing when to compliment another is valuable. Having a balanced view of an opponent is vital for moving toward the next level of play.

Halftime or Post-Game Talk to Opponents

In small groups, ask players to identify and write down three priorities they would have addressed as the visiting coach during halftime or after the game. These comments could include not only tactical approaches by the visitors but also observations of the players' team and how to confront certain strengths or exploit particular weaknesses. The coach may ask the small groups to write down their comment or present them to the team.

Note to Team Member

The day after a game, give your players 3–5 minutes to write a note to a teammate or a member of the team personnel (e.g., trainer, coach, manager) who either contributed positively throughout the game or who had one great moment in the competition. These notes could be delivered.

Video Comments

Did your team have a video taken of the game, match, race, or performance? If so, ask the players to write a blurb of 3–5 sentences to capture and praise the competition as if they were the team's public relations person. Summarizing a game in a paragraph takes a good deal of reflection, especially if one has been a part of that competition.

Best or Most Comical Moments

Throughout any of the notebook pages you'll read thoughtful and comical lines. Every so often, perhaps when your team has a long lay-off or a bye, select some "classic" lines and create a synthesis for a break in the action. Have your players read the collection and then break into small groups to discuss. Finally, in a full team gathering have each small group talk about what players learned, their favorite lines, or the memories that surfaced.

Found Poem

You may discover that having your athletes write a "found poem" begins with "Are you kidding me?" and ends with "Can we do this again?" Honestly, the activity is fun and helps poet-athletes see a game more clearly by thinking more deeply about it. Here are the steps toward creating a Found Poem:

1. Select and photocopy several newspaper articles written about your team or games. Give each of your players one copy—having four or five different articles will produce a variety of poems and make the activity more interesting for all;

2. Give the following directions to your players:
   - Read the article, underline words, phrases or lines that you like or find interesting, put those words, phrases, or lines into a non-rhyming poem that tells the story of the article. Here are a few paragraphs from an article by Kalle Oakes in today's newspaper (*SunJournal,* 11/14/2010) about our hometown football team's victory in the regional playoff championship. I've highlighted words and phrases that I might use in a poem, and then in the poem itself, have put them in an order that feels right to me—I've also added a few of my own words:

     Falcons Squelch Warriors, Win Eighth Regional Title

     RUMFORD — Mountain Valley High School has boasted bigger football teams. More explosive football teams. Teams with more players whose names roll off the tongue in hushed, reverential tones.

     Tough to think of one, offhand, that has played better defense.

     The undefeated, rarely challenged Falcons allowed only five first downs and 87 net yards Saturday in an 18-0 whitewashing of Wells in the Western Class B championship at Chet Bulger Field.

     Here's the opening to the poem:

     EIGHT
     Undefeated
     And rarely challenged—
     Our explosive Falcons
     Whitewashed Wells
     For number eight. . . .

Photo Captions

Tape photographs from competitions or practices onto white paper and ask your players to write captions. Hang the photos around the locker room or at your practice facility. Here are two examples:

One of my former team captains, Peter Rand coaches his son Danny's team. Pete passed along this photograph of his team setting a defensive wall. Danny, with hands up, is on the far right of the wall. The caption? In this case, Pete's comments at the time were perfect: "Cover what's important to you, boys," he hollered. At 10 years old, Pete's son Danny has his own priorities. Do you have a caption for this great picture?

Caption: ______________________________

How about writing a caption for this photograph of Maine Team player, Doug Watt? I took this photo in 1984 just after our dismal *wrong-shoes* loss in England:

Caption: ______________________________

This activity is for the fun of it, but I have to tell you, many interesting conversations occur as a result of the photos.

Theory of Team Development

Many sports such as basketball or water polo require players to learn the team's *system of play* (SOP) as established by the coaching staff (Pruden, 1987). Team Notebooks and Journals can assist with this work.

To guide athletes toward performing effectively within a system of play, team personnel take on certain roles, including the coach as teacher, veteran players as master students, and new players as apprentices (Cheville, 2001). Their work within these roles might include, for example,

- coaches learning about the new players' abilities and personalities;
- veteran players serving as role models for new players;
- new players observing and getting to know veteran players' abilities and personalities;
- veteran players observing and getting to know new players' abilities and personalities;
- all players learning the playbook;
- coaches using a variety of instructional activities to teach the SOP; and
- coaches revising and adapting the team's SOP to more fully match the team's abilities and uniquenesses.

The Theory of Team Development consists of three tiers, or what Pruden calls "Levels of Consciousness" (1987), that players pass through as they come to know their team's system of play (Figure 3.3). Team Notebook pages and activities can play a role in helping coaches teach athletes at Level Two. Notice that Level Two consists of a wide variety of learning experiences such as

practice that consists of play, talk, modeling, and drill,
classroom session that involve lecture, discussion, Q&A, and films, and
playbooks that invite players to read, talk, think, and design plays.

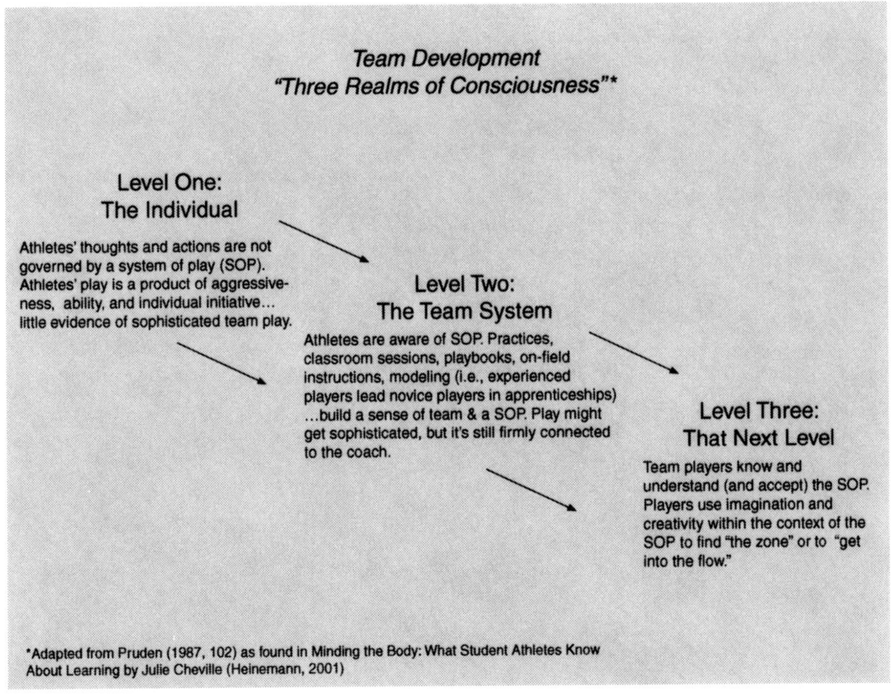

Team Development
"Three Realms of Consciousness"*
Level One:
The Individual
Athletes' thoughts and actions are not governed by a system of play (SOP). Athletes' play is a product of aggressiveness, ability, and individual initiative... little evidence of sophisticated team play.
Level Two:
The Team System
Athletes are aware of SOP. Practices, classroom sessions, playbooks, on-field instructions, modeling (i.e., experienced players lead novice players in apprenticeships) ...build a sense of team & a SOP. Play might get sophisticated, but it's still firmly connected to the coach.
Level Three:
That Next Level
Team players know and understand (and accept) the SOP. Players use imagination and creativity within the context of the SOP to find "the zone" or to "get into the flow."
*Adapted from Pruden (1987, 102) as found in Minding the Body: What Student Athletes Know About Learning by Julie Cheville (Heinemann, 2001)

Figure 3.3 Team Development: "Three Realms of Consciousness"

Now notice in Figure 3.4 how Team Notebook pages and their activities have the potential to complement and supplement what occurs at Level Two. More specifically, the *Competition Analysis I* and its activities assist players in thinking about their team's system of play (SOP). The writing and discussions surrounding the *Competition Analysis II* heighten player understanding and raise consciousness about a team's SOP. Writing provides a unique complement to the day-to-day work of the team and its players; writing has the potential to intensify, recast, and broaden experience in ways that support team development. Essentially, "Writing is a tool for thinking" (College Board, 2003) and the result: deeper learning and better performances.

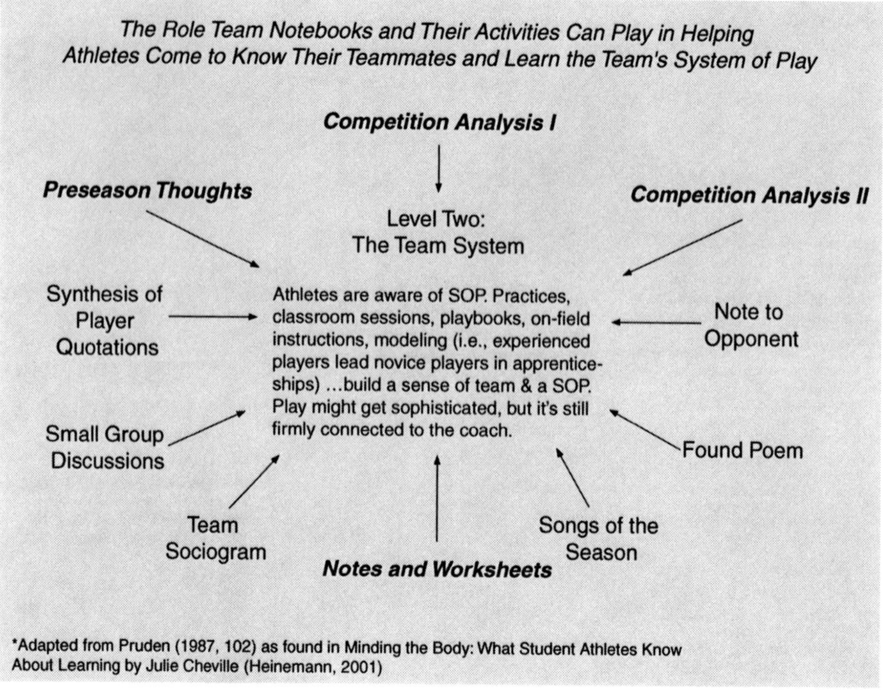

Figure 3.4 The Role of Team Notebooks in Learning a System of Play

And so . . .

Learning from a match, race, or game can be accomplished through athlete-to-athlete conversations, coach-to-athlete discussions, video review, chalk talks, focused practice sessions, drawing and/or recreating plays, lectures from outside expert observers as well as feedback from fans, officials, bench sitters, alumni, sports reporters, friends . . . and writing.

Chapter Four

Competition Analysis II: Telling the Story of Their Game

Writing Manchester United

On a frosty morning in April, my players and I trekked to the outskirts of London for a match made in soccer paradise: Man United vs. Chelsea. As we stepped off the train, all wearing the same navy blue training tops, a horde of hooligans zeroed in on our team. Begging for a brawl, the beer-soaked thugs shoved their chests into our chins. Before I could utter a word to my players, a dozen bobbies swept in and marshaled the twenty of us from the platform. That brief skirmish spiked the boys' adrenaline, and as we scurried to safety through the stadium gate, the teenagers talked smack and glanced over their shoulders.

During the match we sat among a small swarm of wild-eyed supporters of Man United. Their gravelly voices sang their heroes goalward:

Come on you reds, come on you reds
Just keep your bottle and use your heads
For ninety minutes we'll let them know
Who's Man United, here we go.

The action went back and forth with shots and saves until a laser struck from 25 meters settled neatly into the *upper 90* of the goal. The net rippled and we leapt out of our seats, arms jolting high.

As we whisked back into central London on the train, the American teens could not resist chatting up passengers, recounting and reenacting goals, barking out crude stadium songs, mumbling those words that would draw "Coach's look," as they called it. As soccer players and fans, these young athletes had been taken to the promised land of their sport.

An hour after returning to Fitzroy Street, the boys gathered with me in the third floor corridor of the dormitory. They opened their Team Notebooks to a Match Analysis II page. Answering the prompts, the players examined the Man United–Chelsea match. Five minutes into this session, a middle-aged German couple that I'd met at breakfast tiptoed through the silent players whose heads were lowered and pencils pressed into the pages. The couple's eyes met mine. We traded quick smiles as they looked back at the jigsaw of lanky legs and studious boys crisscrossed along the hallway.

Unpacking Other Games

This section of the Team Notebook helps athletes think about a game or match that they have watched together as a team. The game could have been a video in the team room or at a stadium. Either way, the Competition Analysis II is a learning tool that challenges athletes to watch competitions more critically—more fully—and more like coaches than as athlete-participants. To my mind, developing a "coach's eye" as an athlete is the mother lode of learning in sports. Indeed, this analysis page may be my favorite feature of the Team Notebook, and if someone asked me to select just one piece of writing to use with a team, I would move back and forth between the Analysis I and Analysis II.

Not only does an Analysis II help athletes think as coaches, but also this writing front-loads team discussions while highlighting the broad spectrum of tactics and strategies of the competition. In addition, if the competition observed is at a higher level than the athlete's (e.g., high school baseball player watching college game), the writing adds to a player's emerging picture of that next level of play.

In my coaching days before Team Notebooks, I led the team discussions after watching matches together. The discussions, especially when I was a novice coach working with a young team, went something like this: I asked a question, some players answered, I commented, and I asked something else. In terms of learning, this approach suppressed some players' exploratory thinking, not only by the questions I asked, but also by using a large group, question-and-answer format. Not all of us feel comfortable or think clearly when speaking in large-group settings. That's especially true for novice or shy players—or for that matter inexperienced coaches.

In the end, coaches usually possess a more complete view of a game because of our years of experience and educational backgrounds. Helping players see that "more complete view" is complicated work and demands that we move beyond a question-and-answer session that assumes all athletes learn by observing and being quizzed. Players who lack experience don't often see the more complex picture of team play. They get caught up in scoring plays or focus on their counterparts (e.g., goalkeeper commenting on goalkeeper). A Q&A session won't destroy a team, in fact the activity might showcase more experienced players' understandings and that may motivate the younger or less experienced players. However, most players need more guidance and support (i.e., scaffolding) through the thinking and learning process. The prompts provided in the Competition Analysis II pages will help with that work.

How the Analysis II Came About

The Analysis II happened because my large-group team discussions just didn't work well. Indeed, I saw too many silent players who felt uncomfortable and too many confident players dominating the stage. Over time I began varying my approach. After watching a video or attending a college match, I put players in small groups to discuss the game. Usually, I divided up my soccer team discussions by offense, midfield, and defense. The players would talk about the match we observed; they'd use chart paper to record three to five observations of the game; and then we'd gather in a larger group to share what had been discussed. Each of the smaller groups had one spokesperson who talked about the chart paper for the rest of the members. I believe this approach brought more athletes into the discussions, but I still felt like some players were not involved.

To make sure everyone took part, I asked athletes to take a few minutes to write a summary of the match we watched. Often, those summaries told the story of the game but did not go into specifics. Here's a summary by Eric Swallow who played on a state level team that toured in England:

> Millwall edged Wolverhampton 1-0 in a close match on Wednesday night. The game remained scoreless throughout the first half, partly because Millwall's offense was time consuming and ground based, and partly because the Wolves' chips and long passes weren't on the mark. Late in the 2nd half the deadlock was broken by Mitchell of Millwall on a head ball just outside of the six from a cross by John Kerr. Wolverhampton had some good scoring opportunities late in the game, but they couldn't convert, and the Millwall side and its fans returned home triumphant.

Pieces of writing like Eric's led me to developing the prompts for the Analysis II. I also immediately created a series of writing activities to complement this notebook page. I say "created," but really many of these activities mirrored what I did in my high school classroom and now use in my graduate school classroom.

Preparing athletes for group discussions by having them write an Analysis II will be a valuable addition to the learning that takes place on a team. Here are some ways of using the Analysis II with a team:

- *Next Level Games:* When middle schoolers attend a high school game or when a college team attends a professional match, players may use the Analysis II to help unpack a competition.
- *Tournaments:* During a tournament select one game to observe and write about. You may wish to choose a game that includes a

team (or teams) you play during the regular season or may play in postseason. If a particularly dynamic team is participating at the tournament, one that your team will never play, you may want to select that team for the pure learning value. Jonathan's analysis in Figure 4.1 includes one team from our own high school conference and another outside of our conference.

- *First Team←→Second Team:* Your club or school may field first and second teams (i.e., varsity and JV). Once a season the first team could watch and analyze the second team's match using the Analysis II. The second team should have the same opportunity.
- *Team homework:* Your players may love this homework more than any other they've been assigned. Have them watch a professional match at home or with friends and then complete an Analysis II on the game. Coach Nick Miller did just that with *Super Bowl XLV* 2011. The Coach does well at disguising his lifelong love of the Green Bay Packers (Figure 4.2).

Activities to Use with the Analysis II

There are a number of activities from previous Team Notebook pages that athletes and teams might use with the Analysis II. Likewise, the following activities may be adapted for other pages:

Listening In

A team discussion activity called "Listening In" takes place in a training session after a varsity (first team) watches a junior varsity (second) team play a game—or vice versa—this example features soccer:

- The team that *observed* the match separates into groups of forwards, midfielders, and defenders/keepers. Players discuss the match for 10–15 minutes using their individual Analysis II as guides.
- The coach calls the three groups together and leads them in a discussion about the match they observed.

Match Analysis II

Player: Jonathan

Torrance High School	**Freedom High School**
Alignment of Players: 4-4-2	*Alignment of Players:* 4-4-2 1st half, 4-3-3 2nd half
Strengths: Outside midfielders made great runs.	*Strengths:* Sweeper, Center Mid
Weaknesses: They seemed to relax when they were up 2-0.	*Weaknesses:* Young. Didn't use space well.
Half-time adjustments: None. They came out flat. Overconfident.	*Half-time adjustments:* Went to a 4-3-3 to get more targets up front.

General Comments:

Torrance High School	Freedom High School
Forwards: Fast	Forwards: Lacked movement
Midfielders: Athletic	Midfielders: Lost composure—their talk was not constructive.
Defenders: Moved well together.	Defenders: Seemed spacey. Lost track of play.
Keeper: Confident—great technique—team leader.	Keeper: Poor positioning. No Talk. Cried after 2nd goal.

Figure 4.1 Competition Analysis II (soccer) (*continued*)

Team #1 Man of the Match: Why?	*Team #2 Man of the Match:* Why?
#6—left mid. His runs through the D opened up huge space. He always encouraged his mates. He's the kind of player I'd like to be. Great goal.	Sweeper—he kept his cool. It's not easy managing younger players.

Moment of the Match:

#6's run through the D and his one-touch to the near post. Sweet String Music! Magic!

Final Analysis:

Think as a coach about team strengths (e.g., athleticism, speed, coaching, motivation/ heart) and weaknesses. What adjustments might you have made to either team if you were that team's coach?

THS needed to work on the simple things: move to space and play the way you face. They were a lot younger than FHS and just needed to try to play within themselves. It's like you told us over the last 2 years. Play the fundamentals—it's a simple game so keep it that way. As for FHS, they didn't stay focused for the whole match. Their coach needed to teach not yell—the guy embarrassed himself.

Figure 4.1 *(continued)*

- The team that played in the match sits outside the discussion and listens in. Those players may wish to take notes in their Team Notebook while listening.
- After the discussion, the team that listened leaves to discuss their match using both their observation notes from the discussion and their Analysis I sheets.
- The rules of "Listening In" are clear-cut: Players analyzing the match are cautioned not to single out one player's performance, good or bad, or to critique the coach. The team being critiqued listens in and is not allowed to speak. The activity demands maturity and trust.

Red Riot Football
Game Analysis II
by *Coach Nick Miller*
NFL Super Bowl 2011

Team #1 **Green Bay Packers**

Offensive System
lots of 3-wide sets, some I, some bone

Strengths
completed passes outside of numbers for big yardage, converted 3rd downs early

Weaknesses
few rushing attempts, dropped key passes

Defensive System
base 3-4, played a lot of nickel 2-4-5

Strengths
forced game changing turnovers, overcame injury to #21 Woodson, held up on 4th down of Pittsburgh's final drive

Weaknesses
struggled to stop the run because they lost contain

Half-time adjustments
all but abandoned run game, blitzed #24 from the slot in Woodson's absence

Team #2 **Pittsburgh Steelers**

Offensive System
mostly ace, some double tight, some bunch trips

Strengths
ran the ball well to right side with LG #63 pulling, had more time of possession

Weaknesses
lost the turnover battle, failed to exploit injury in Packer secondary

Defensive System
primarily 3-4, lots of cover 2

Strengths
front seven stopped the run game early and got pressure on the QB Rodgers

Weaknesses
gave up big pass plays on vertical routes up the seam and outside the numbers, no takeaways

Half-time adjustments
threw to #17 Wallace more often, but overall very few adjustments, just better execution

Figure 4.2 Coach Miller's Analysis II of Super Bowl *XLV* 2011 (*continued*)

Backfield
Starks ran hard when given the opportunity, all Backs picked up the blitz well, QB Rodgers was unstoppable

Receivers
somehow managed to make up for inexcusable drops with big plays for touchdowns, relentless

Offensive Line
very solid on the interior, allowed to much pressure on the edges

Defensive Line
quiet for most of the night, but kept the QB in the pocket and forced one of the picks

Linebackers
inside backers made tackles from sideline to sideline, outside backers poor against run (Got hooked on outside run plays) but made key plays (Zombo's sack and Matthews' forced fumble)

Secondary/Defensive Backfield
stepped up when their leader and best player went down, made great interceptions and shut down the passing game on Pitt's final drive

Team #1 Player of the Game:
Quarterback Aaron Rodgers
Why?
One of the greatest Super Bowl Performances by a QB ever. Took the team on his shoulders And outplayed his counterpart With 3 TD passes and over 300 yards

Backfield
Mendenhall ran through the through the Packer defense, QB Roethlisberger threw crippling picks

Receivers
made the plays when they were thrown to

Offensive Line
run blocking was dominant

Defensive Line
helped shut down the run but got very little pressure up the middle

Linebackers
strength of the D, outside backers were effective rushing the passer, outside and inside were tough against the run

Secondary/Defensive Backfield
outmatched by Packer receivers, Polamalu is a playmaker when around the line of scrimmage but Packer's formations forced him to drop into coverage

Team #2 Player of the Game:
RB Rashard Mendenhall
Why?
gashed Packer D for big chunks of Yards, best run of the game was his TD run, Pitt made a mistake in not giving him the ball more often

Figure 4.2 *(continued)*

Moment of the Game

The Packer's Clay Matthews forced a fumble from RB Rashard Mendenhall that was scooped up by Desmond Bishop of the Packers. This killed Pittsburgh's momentum and they did not score again after this.

Final Analysis

The Packer's strength was clearly their passing attack. Rodgers proved he is an elite QB, and the receivers caused mismatches for the Steeler's secondary. Rodgers' cannon arm and accuracy allowed him to tear up the Steeler's D and make plays to his receivers, whose precise route running and knowledge of the opposing D allowed them to get open. As a team they showed great resiliency when two veteran leaders in Charles Woodson and Donald Driver were injured. If I was a coach I may have blitzed Roethlisberger more often to try and disrupt some of their long scoring drives.

The Steeler's defense has been dominant the entire year, even with an average secondary. Their studs in the front seven played well, but the secondary was exposed. Polamalu played about as poor as the NFL's Defensive Player of the Year could. Their Super Bowl experience allowed them to make a run at a comeback when they were down 21-3, but they turned the ball over three times which led to 21 points for Green Bay. It's nearly impossible to win when a team does this. They showed a lack of discipline when they committed penalties that negated big special teams plays. If I were coaching the Steelers I would have given the ball to the running backs more often. They were gaining great yardage and controlling the clock.

Figure 4.2 (*continued*)

Group Work after Watching Game Films

For this activity you may use your team's game films or videos from next level of play (e.g., college, professional), the Analysis II provides a mechanism for all players to reflect on a match. After the film, give players a few minutes to write the analysis. To change it up a bit, you may wish to group players by positions or year in school. Ask them to fill out one Analysis II as a group.

Discussing and Selecting the Player of the Game

On the Analysis II page, players are asked to identify their choice of Player of the Game. In addition, your players will give reasons for their selection. The following activity uses those results:

1. Divide your athletes into small groups with teammates who selected the same Player of the Match.

2. Have them discuss the player's qualities using their Analysis II comments. Ask a player to keep notes on the qualities discussed.
3. Ask each small group to create a poster that highlights their player's strengths as well as the major difference the player offered in the competition.
4. Place the posters on a class- or locker-room wall and ask the groups to move from poster to poster to discuss the merits of each Player of the Game nominee.
5. Have a full team discussion on each nominee and at the end, pass out paper and take a vote on the Player of the Game.

If you want to add a bit of competition to this subjective activity, ask a former player, the athletic director, a coach from another sport, or the team captains to judge the posters on the strength of observations. The most effective poster wins a trip to Disneyland (No, I'm not serious). Depending on the ability of your players, you may also have the small groups, or a selected individual from each "camp," discuss the qualities of their selection in front of the whole team and welcome a debate.

Sportscaster Commentary

Ask players to bring their laptops or a recording device to practice. Have small groups of players write summaries of the match much like Eric Swallow did with the Millwall vs. Wolverhampton match above. Then, ask them to fine-tune the summary into a sports caster's commentary. Have one player record the commentary and ultimately play the final pieces for the entire team. Vote on the favorite and give an award.

Reenactments

In small or large groups, have team members select highlights from the game (e.g., scoring plays, defensive plays) and create a reenactment replete with a script that showcases the various components of the play. Usually, this kind of activity will take place at the field, court, pool, or arena, and as much as this is fun, the accompanying script will help teammates see more clearly the "pieces" of a great score or sound defense. This activity is a lot like a coach's chalk-talk . . . the difference is, as with all of these activities: the players are in charge.

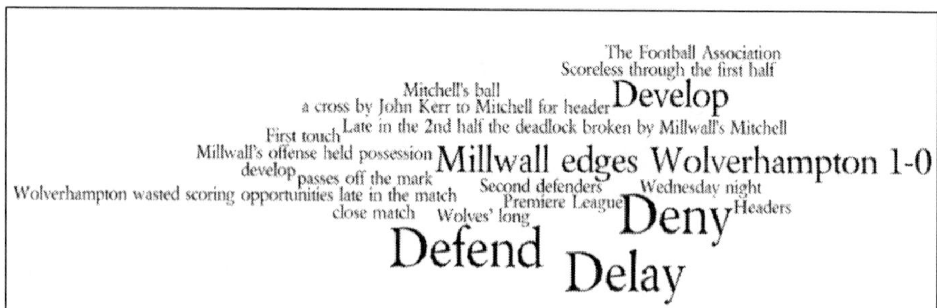

Figure 4.3 Word Clouds, Millwall Professional Soccer Match

The Art of Creating Word Clouds

Using players' laptops or the school's computer lab have athletes work in pairs. Ask them to select words from their Analysis IIs. Using a free online word cloud program like Wordle (www.wordle.net) create a word-art interpretation of the match (Figure 4.3). You'll be intrigued watching your athletes create word clouds. The players get hooked on the process and on revising the final product. Most important of all, however, you'll be fascinated at the conversations that unfold during the process of selecting and highlighting the words to use in the artwork. You'll hear discussions about the game as they determine which words to emphasize. Then, when the word clouds are shared—hung in the team room or passed from group to group—the players' observations and game talk will surprise you.

And so . . .

As a learning tool, the Competition Analysis II can challenge all levels of athletes to watch their sports with a more critical eye. The models provided here are basic. Why not explore the possibilities of the Analysis II by creating prompts or questions for your sport that will push athletes to explore a competition more fully and in different ways. Even more, why not invite your senior players or position players (offense/defense) to come up with their own versions of the Analysis II. Such an assignment is akin to having athletes design their own training sessions or game plans—they have to think broadly, beyond themselves, like coaches.

Chapter Five

Postseason Thoughts: Looking Back, Thinking Forward, and Making Plans . . . Again

"I like to have my student-athletes write about their experiences, be it about practice, a game, or even an injury. Writing helps them to analyze their play, thought processes, and feelings. It brings more meaning to what they are experiencing. Writing . . . is a reminder of what we all are playing for and working towards."

–Coach Nicole Moore, University of Vermont

Finding Closure

Our first soccer banquet took place in another school's parking lot after the final game of our inaugural season. Gallon jugs of supermarket fruit juice along with bologna, American cheese, white bread, and potato chips were laid out on the trunk of my '76 Ford Torino Limited. Homemade chocolate chip cookies baked by the moms who had driven our high school club to every match proved to be the highlight. That first year, all of our games were away. No trophies or athletic letters were awarded during our club's parking-lot celebration, but the players savored the win, that season, and those cookies.

Postseason Thoughts

"This year I really felt like I led the *team*."

And he had. Jonathan's Postseason Thoughts (Figure 5.1) reveal his growth as player, leader, and person. By midseason, he emerged as an on-field captain even though he did not wear the armband. The next season, his senior year, he would captain our side.

During our one-on-one debriefing session after the season, Jonathan and I spoke about his need to earn money for college. That discussion led us to talk about his potential to play at the next level. We also reviewed the winter indoor season and discussed recruiting players, especially 8th graders, for those evening games. Jonathan understood the value of indoor play in the off-season and also committed to summer soccer. Another discussion focused on Jonathan's perceived weakness in dealing with players who "make excuses and whine about everything."

As is evident in Jonathan's writing, Postseason Thoughts help athletes think broadly and look forward. For those players who will return to the team the next season, writing Postseason Thoughts kicks off the new season many months in advance. This writing can help athletes organize their off-season training and may eliminate those blank spaces in the next year's Preseason Thoughts.

Some coaches conduct postseason debriefs with athletes to review the previous season and to prepare for the next. Using an athlete's Postseason Thoughts as a guide will assist with that discussion. These pages also serve as motivation for some players. For coaches who mail team letters home to athletes at the midpoint between seasons, the copy of Postseason Thoughts will allow the coach to write personal notes about the athlete's goals for the upcoming season. Such reminders can jump-start players who have stalled with their training goals.

Activities

As with the other pages of the Team Notebooks, the Postseason Thoughts allow for a variety of activities to help work toward your athletes' deeper understanding.

Postseason Thoughts
Player: Jonathan

My strengths this season as a player:

Last year I felt like I directed the defense pretty well. This year I really felt like I led the team. It's such a cool feeling to be able to "orchestrate" (thanks for the word) an attack. I saw the full field—I knew what to say and how to say it—I felt confident with the ball—I loved the one-on-one moments with great players. Ryan and I worked well together.

My weaknesses this season as a player:

I made some bad decisions during matches and I let those decisions get to me. I dropped my head at Winthrop after I got beat for the goal. In OT or the end of some games, sometimes I felt tired. Like you said, I need to think about preserving my energy. I don't like players who make excuses and cry about everything. I have to learn to talk with them better.

In the off-season here's what I plan to do to improve as a player for the next season:

Train! I've got the whole year planned and I'll show it to you in our debrief. I'm playing indoor with Central. Ryan and I designed a weight program we're going to be HUGE! Summer camp to be sure. I'll co-coach community center soccer—I have to work more hours this summer College $$$.

When I review the goals I set for myself at the beginning of the season in my notebook, here's how I think I did:

I wrote about talk, composure, and leadership on and off the pitch. I feel good about everything except off-field leadership. I have to learn to talk with kids who aren't into it. They just bug me.

This year our team strengths included:

- We had good movement off the ball
- Good talk
- Positive attitude (most of us)
- Seniors
- Making the finals and playing tough.
- Great pregame, good stretching

This year our team weaknesses included:

- Seniors—haha, just kidding. I'll miss them.
- Maybe we're too polite some times. I know—we'll have to talk about this one.
- Playing quicker . . . that will come with age.

Figure 5.1 Postseason Thoughts (soccer) (*continued*)

Here's how I am doing in my classes this season:

Classes	How I'm doing:
Pre-Calculus	B (I'll get an A 2nd Q)
Physics	B+
Writing Center English	A (This class is easy. Ha!)
US History	A
Psychology	A+

Other thoughts:

How about a 2 day minicamp in preseason at the lake? Ryan and I will organize it. It'll be great for getting everybody together. Thanks for everything, Coach. See you in English!

Offseason Contact Information:

Player: Jonathan Grade: 11 Phone: 364.2953

Email: *jonathan@email.com*

Parents/Guardians: *Rylee and Christian*

Address: *Porter Avenue*

Parent/Guardian Email: *home@email.com*

Figure 5.1 (*continued*)

Study Guide/Writing Prompt

This activity may be used with any Team Notebook page. Notebook pages from past seasons may function as study guides and/or writing prompts for players in subsequent seasons. Important: Be careful not to use any writing that may be hurtful and make sure your players know that their writing may be used in this manner with future teams. Here are several examples:

- Postseason Thoughts from years past may be used with current players to help them think more deeply about their positions. For example, after reading Jonathan's Postseason Thoughts in this chapter, sweeper Zach Taylor took 8 minutes to think and write about his own role as a central defender:

  As a seasoned sweeper, I found myself struggling to pull my team together at times. I can relate completely to a team weakness of being too polite. There are times to be nice and there are times that you must get your point across. As a sweeper, you are the leader on the field—you must tell your teammates where to be and when to be there. It takes an immense amount of leadership to corral ten men to follow your orders. When one man falters we all falter. Being a sweeper is a defensive position but the weight of your team sites on your shoulders. Sweepers are beacons of light. They rally the troops. Above all else, a sweeper needs to keep his head on straight.

- When a new player comes on to the team, provide the athlete with Postseason Thoughts, samples of other pages, or a complete Team Notebook from the previous season. New players may find reading the Postseason Thoughts especially helpful in understanding the role and expectations of certain positions. Providing a model Team Notebook to new players will help elevate the importance of writing on your team. In addition, supplying a model may help those athletes who struggle with writing.
- Use Competition Analysis I pages from the previous year as pregame study guides. In effect, the previous year's Team Notebooks become a kind of textbook. Obviously, players and coaches from the competition change from year to year, but programs often tend to have similar philosophies of play. Your players will have an opportunity to discuss a competition's trends and approaches by reviewing the previous year's Analysis I. It's a great way to focus on an upcoming game.

What Helped You Learn This Season?

Perhaps this activity is as much for the coach as it is for the athlete. During one of the final practices of the season, ask players to review their Team Notebooks and to make a list of the activities and experiences that served as the most effective learning moments of the season. For example, as a result of attending college games as high school players, athletes may list the "team discussions" that occurred after the games. Perhaps the team gathered to watch a championship game on TV and the follow-up activity had players "pairing up to fill out the Analysis II." Such comments will be used to create a chart that showcases the ways your players learned. For a model, look back at Figure 1, "Some of the Ways Athletes Learn," in the book's introduction.

Synthesis of Quotations

Ask your players to select two or three of their most meaningful lines from Postseason Thoughts or any of the Team Notebook pages. Place these quotations into a synthesis to share during the final days of practice or to be read at the awards banquet. Such a reading allows every player's thoughts to be heard and surely reinforces the notion of "team." Be sure not to include entries that could be hurtful to teammates or others. Finally, if the players didn't already, it's fun for the coach to include a few common expressions, especially the phrases players might repeat in a playful way (e.g., "OK, Gentleman, if you would be so kind . . . to the baseline.").

If you'd like to orchestrate a Reading-in-the-Round for the year-end banquet, follow these simple directions and use Figure 5.2 as a guide:

- Select six senior players and assign each one a number 1–6.
- Take the collection you've typed out and number each quotation using a shuffling effect (e.g., 1-3-6-2-4-5-3-1-2-6-5-4 . . .); the shuffling of numbers will create a crisscross effect when the players read their lines.
- Print out seven copies of the synthesis so you have one as a backup.
- Practice the reading before the banquet.
- Remind your players that when they read their lines to speak clearly, to pause if there's laughter, and to ham it up when appropriate.
- Play soft music in the background, if desired.

Senior Letters

Coach Brian Bold of Burnt Hills HS has his graduating players write letters to the entire team. As you'll see in Figure 5.3, Coach Bold has his players read the letters during the postseason matches and at the end-of-season banquet.

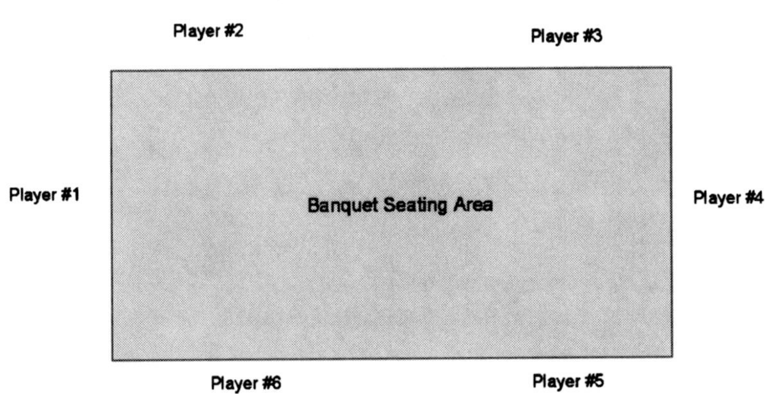

Figure 5.2 Reading-in-the-Round Set-up

Tradition Never Graduates
Burnt Hills Women Soccer

Senior Letters

The tradition of Postseason Senior Letters began a few years ago within the Burnt Hills varsity soccer program. They have been a source of motivation and reflection for players. These letters have brought out both tears and smiles for many teams over the years. Senior letters are designed for our players to look back and reflect on the soccer program, their experiences and memories while playing at BH-BL. Players have added quotes, included stories (sad, inspiring and humorous) and even pictures to their letters. These letters can take any form that you feel would be appropriate in describing your years wearing maroon and white. My goal is for these letters to be read aloud to the team prior to postseason matches and at end of season banquet to provide a means of reflection and motivation. Please type out your letter, give it some time and much thought, because your audience will truly be listening. I would like all Senior Letters to be handed in to me by Friday, October 29th.

Thanks,
Coach Bold

Figure 5.3 Senior Letters

Letters to Incoming Athletes

During the off-season, assign your veteran athletes an incoming athlete to write a letter to. These letters welcome newcomers, of course, but writing also gives veteran athletes an opportunity to think *again* about the team and their off-season preparation. Here's the opening paragraph from senior Ryan Goodwin's letter to incoming 8th graders:

> *I am writing to tell you a little about my experience with Falcon Soccer over the past three years. During this time, I have grown to realize that the Falcons are known as a skilled team, but more importantly, we are known for having fun while we play. Falcon Soccer has a reputation of playing properly and fair, but also playing hard. This style of play has been recognized and appreciated by many of the teams in our league.*

With these letters, coaches often include a New Athlete Information Form. This form gathers background material while giving these new athletes an opportunity to write and reflect on their schooling, sport, and new team. The responses also serve as a warm-up to Team Notebooks. Here are sample prompts for a New Athlete Information Form:

Describe yourself as a student (e.g., favorite classes, grades for each 8th-grade class).

Describe yourself as a soccer player (e.g., years played, positions played, soccer camps attended, honors received).

How do you spend your free time?

What other sports do you participate in?

If you've ever been to a Falcon Soccer varsity match, describe the team's play. What are the differences in play from middle school to high school?

Again, if you've seen the Falcons play, who is your favorite player on the high school team right now and why?

Describe any plans you may have once you graduate from high school.

Tell us something about you as a person, student, and player that we should know.

"How Might Writing Make You a Faster Ski Racer?"

If you're wondering how writing works with your athletes, ask them. After the ski racers of Burke Mountain Academy returned from 3-weeks of October training in Chile, I asked how writing in their journals might make them faster ski racers. Here are three responses from the 15- and 16-year-old skiers:

> Writing makes you learn about yourself. Knowing yourself physically and mentally as an athlete is very important. Writing made me think about what I was doing well and what I need to work on. This will make my training and motivation much better. Writing down what I need to work on after video was really helpful for me.
>
> —Chris McKenna

> Writing does a lot for me. It helps me organize my thoughts. In ski racing, there can be hundreds of different things I could be doing right and another hundred I could be doing wrong. Keeping track of all these things in my mind is a hard task. To write the things that went well or the things that went not so well at the end of each day is extremely helpful.
>
> –Griffin Brown

> Skiing is a sport where the mind plays an important role. It is very technique-based and sometimes your problems are a lack of understanding. Writing forces you to maintain thought once you leave the hill. A coach once said to me that to become a skier that gets the most out of training, your mind cannot turn off once the day is over. Writing helps with that. Constant reflection enforces understanding.
>
> –Sam Coffin

End-of-the-Season Journal

Prompt your athletes to write about the season in a journal. Here, Matt Kellogg writes about his final game with Sal, his long-time baseball teammate:

> *I've been playing with Sal Mazza since I was eight years old, and that was our last game together. . . . While I've pretty much stayed at shortstop over the years, Sal's been in a number of different positions all around me. I've cheered him on while he was*

> *pitching, turned double plays when he's at second, and thrown over to him at first. I've taken his cut-offs to the plate from left field and stood with him on the left side of the infield when he plays third. In the bottom of our last inning together, that's where we were, Sal at third and me at short. I told him that this would be our last time playing together. During the inning, Sal and I both made nice fielding plays, a good way to end a baseball career together. . . . I'm looking forward to next year as I plan to get back on top of this damn league and turn some heads.*

This kind of thinking captures moments past while setting the groundwork for the next season.

And so . . .

Ending the year with Postseason Thoughts adds a unique element to your team's learning and experience. Writing the reflection can bring closure to a season while helping athletes and coaches think about the next. Similar to Preseason Thoughts, this reflection provides opportunities for widespread discussions and meaningful deliberations.

Chapter Six

Notes, Worksheets, and Activities

Although my players got a kick out of writing on those airsickness bags when we flew home from England, there are times when a blank piece of paper is helpful. As with other sections of the Team Notebook, the Notes pages may be expanded or modified to accommodate your program's needs. As a result, this section also includes sample worksheets and activities that help athletes unpack and organize their thinking.

Notes Pages

Just Notes

Instead of plain paper, you might want to photocopy your mascot or team name on the page. For certain sports, having a photocopy of the field of play could prove useful as in Figure 6-1. Players can take Notes in the margin or on the field of play. On the reverse side include space for more notes or in the case of sports with designed plays (e.g., basketball, water polo), include "the red zone" on two sides of the

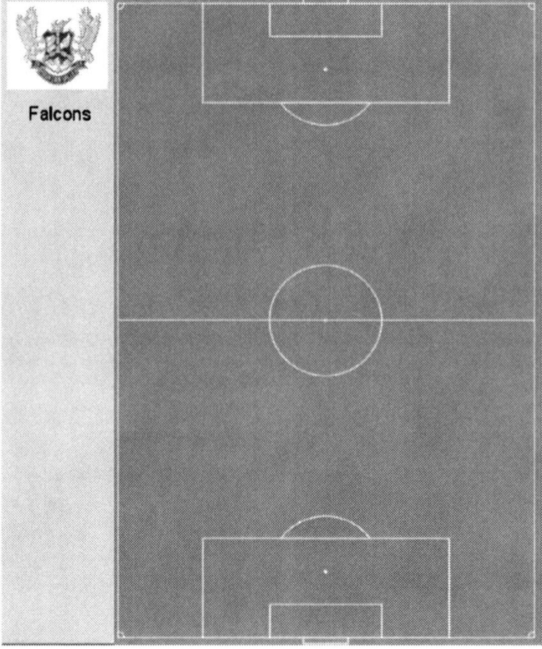

Figure 6.1 Front page of Notes (Sport: soccer)

paper (see Figure 6.2). Obviously, there are countless versions of this two-sided sheet that you or your players could create. In fact, why not put your players to work at designing sheets such as these.

Opponent's Highlights and Notes

Local and regional newspapers often feature preseason highlights for teams. Photocopy previews of your competition and include those write-ups in the notes section as I have demonstrated in Figure 6-3. In the lined space provided, you could ask your athletes to write their thoughts about the team previews or use the space for notes or activities.

Program History

You may want to include highlights from your program's history at the beginning of the Team Notebook. Include the overall program

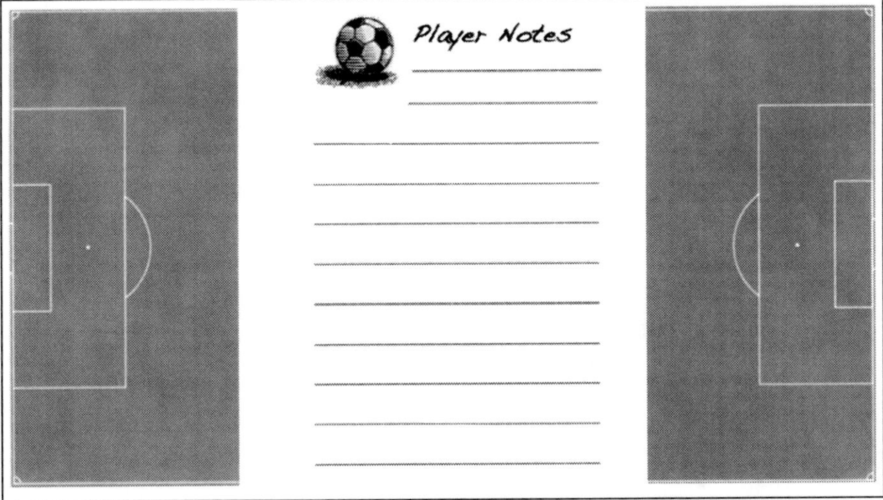

Figure 6.2 Back page of Notes (Sport: soccer)

record or awards received. You might choose to spread those program highlights throughout the notebook. A Notes page of award-winning players throughout the years shows that a "team" is a part of a much larger program. One example for your Notes section is illustrated in Figure 6.4.

Riverside Wrestling

Coach: Shawn Walek (14th year)

Returning letter winners: Seniors — Kyle Roads, Eric Meader, Pat Sirois, Tyler Carmack; Juniors — Matt Meader, Tammy Smiley; Sophomores — Dalton White, Tyler McCarthy;

Promising newcomers: Freshman — Stewart Smyth.

Outlook: The Eagles went .500 last year because they went into every meet with two or three holes, sometimes more with injuries or illness. An influx of new talent has the numbers strong enough this year that they should have every weight class filled except 103. Carmack and Pat Meader qualified for states last year, and Roads could join them this year. Sirois finished third among Class C heavy weights last year.

Coach's comment: "I'm excited because we have a lot of freshmen and a lot of new guys." — Coach Shawn Walek

Figure 6.3 Opponent's Highlights Notes Page

NOTES

KJ ANASTASIO, '89
-All New England
-All State
-All Conference
-Maine Senior Bowl

DAN GARBARINI, '91
-All New England
-All State
-All Conference
-Maine Senior Bowl

SHAWN HUNT, '92
-All State
-All Conference
-Maine Senior Bowl

FRED KENT, '93
-All State
-All Conference
-Maine Senior Bowl

DEAN BOUDREAU, '93
-All State
-All Conference
-Maine Senior Bowl

IAN GARBARINI, '93
-All State
-All Conference
-Maine Senior Bowl

Figure 6.4 History Page Notes Page

Rules of the Game

The rules you include on a Notes page will depend on the age and experience of your athletes. More experienced players might value more complicated or obscure rules. In some Team Notebooks, coaches choose to include a separate rules section at the beginning of the Notebook. See Figure 6.5 for one example of Rules of the Game Notes Page.

Sports Quotations

Whether motivational, humorous, or instructional, sports quotations make an interesting sidebar for a Notes page (Figure 6.6).

NOTES

GROUND RULE TRIPLES
A ground rule triple, in which three bases are awarded to a batter who hits a fair ball, can occur in one of two ways: A fielder deliberately touches the ball with his hat or mask in an attempt to catch the ball, or a fielder deliberately throws his glove at a fair ball (and/or a thrown glove hits a fair ball).

PITCHING A SHUTOUT
Baseball rule 10.9 (f) states that a pitcher will not be credited with pitching a shutout unless he completes the game. The second part of this rule states that if a pitcher enters the game in the first inning with no outs before the opposing team scores and gets out of the inning without a run scored and then pitches the rest of the game without giving up a run he shall be credited with a shutout.

BASE RUNNING ASSISTANCE
Baseball rule 5.10 states that if an accident happens to a runner that prevents him from proceeding to a base to which he is entitled (such as on a home run), a substitute runner shall be permitted to complete the play.

Figure 6.5 Rules of the Game Notes Page

I've missed more than 9000 shots in my career. I've lost almost 300 games. 26 times, I've been trusted to take the game winning shot and missed. I've failed over and over and over again in my life. And that is why I succeed.
—Michael Jordan

My motto was always to keep swinging. Whether I was in a slump or feeling badly or having trouble off the field, the only thing to do was keep swinging.
—Hank Aaron

One of the things that my parents have taught me is never listen to other people's expectations. You should live your own life and live up to your own expectations, and those are the only things I really care about it. **—Tiger Woods**

We are what we repeatedly do. Excellence, therefore, is not an act but a habit. **—Aristotle**

Figure 6.6 Sports Quotations Notes Page

Worksheets and Activities

Graphic Organizers

A graphic organizer guides athletes in thinking about an opponent, their team, and their play. Athletes like using graphic organizers because the blocks of writing make visible their thoughts. Such pages can provide a five-minute warm-up activity to a team-wide discussion about an upcoming competition or a team issue. Figures 6.7, 6.8, and 6.9 are sample graphic organizers that, in 3–5 minutes, will help athletes focus their thinking.

Graphic organizers are interesting to create because what you're attempting to do is mine your athletes' thoughts. In addition, these tools prove effective with athletes who are visual learners and for athletes who need a bit more of a framework when writing.

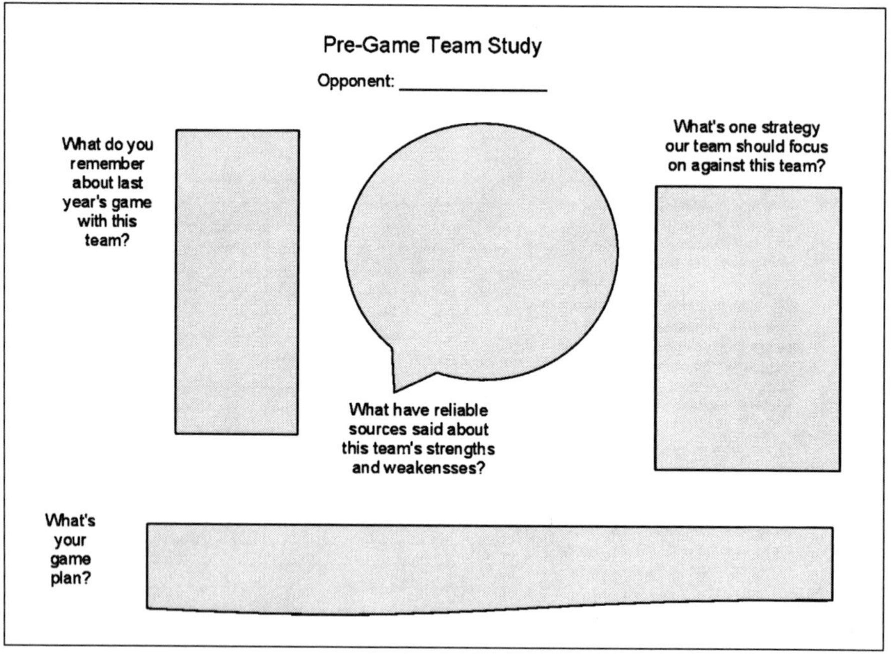

Figure 6.7 Pre-Game Team Study Activity

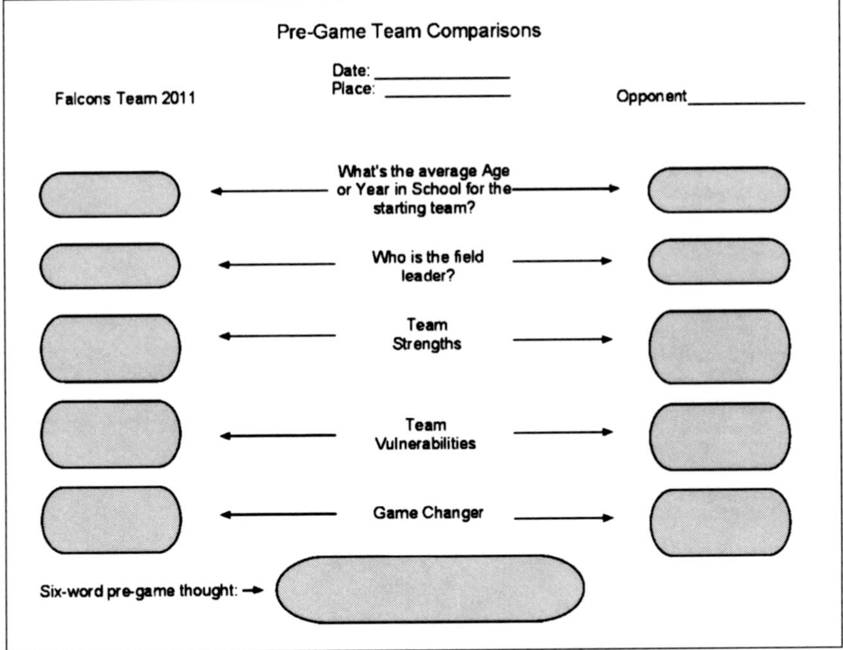

Figure 6.8 Pre-Game Team Comparison Activity

Opponent: __________________

Date: ______________________

Always as a player I must

Finally as a team we must...

Then as a team we must..

Next as a team we must...

First, as a team we must...

Figure 6.9 Steps to Playing Well as a Team

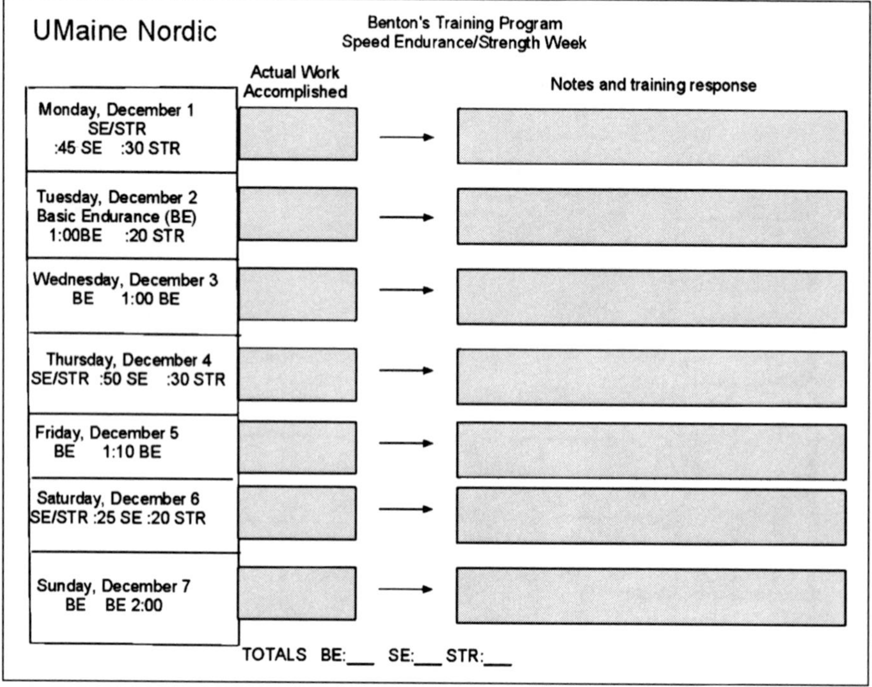

Figure 6.10 Team Calendar, Individual Athlete's Training Plan with Notes

Calendar

Include a weekly calendar with an area for notes to one side. I've included an example from a Nordic ski racer. What's different from team sports like basketball or baseball is that cross-country skiing athletes, like runners, have individualized training plans designed for their particular levels of experience and capacity (Figure 6.10). This addition will serve as a reference for athletes as well as space to write and reflect. The backside of the calendar has space for journaling and notes.

The second example in Figure 6.11 showcases a calendar that prompts team athletes to respond to practices, matches, and recovery days. Once again, the backside of the calendar provides space for general notetaking.

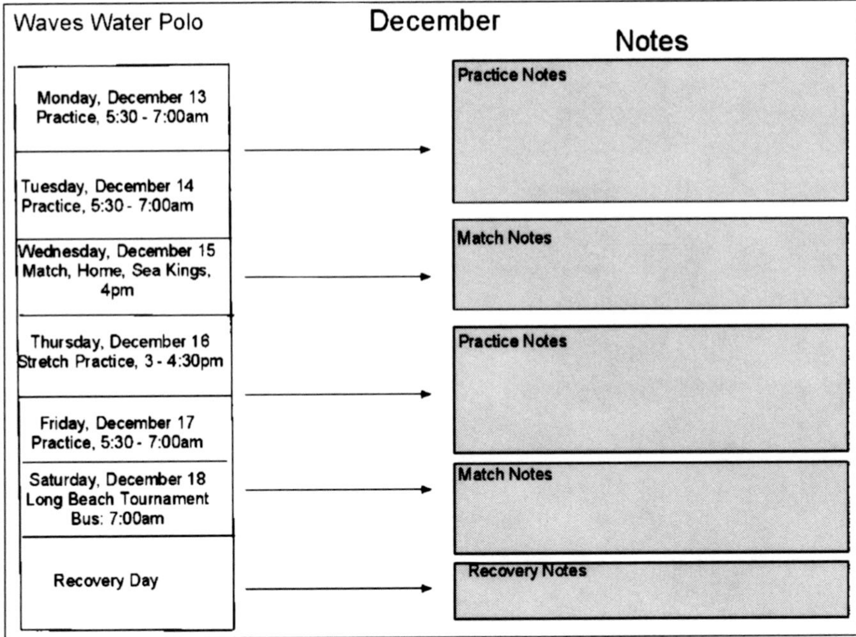

Figure 6.11 Team Calendar, Individual Athlete's Notes

And so . . .

By now you've probably thought of a number of Notes page sidebars for your specific sport or program needs. Maybe you'll include pages of sports trivia or create a contest for your athletes based on your program's history. As always, the key is to make the Notes pages, and Team Notebooks themselves, useful for you and your athletes.

Chapter Seven

Athletes' Journals

From Wimbledon to Fenway Park

A journal provides an athlete with a place to set goals, reflect, grapple with issues, keep track of training ideas, and record results as well as plan, scheme, ponder, rant, question, draw, and rejoice. As with Team Notebooks, there is no one right way to utilize these books. Athletes like Serena Williams use their journal writing for motivation and focusing. During Wimbledon 2007, the two-time champion pulled out her journal book and shared her musings with the press (Figure 7.1).

During the mid-2000s, Red Sox pitching ace Curt Schilling could be seen on the bench between innings writing notes on the pitches he delivered to certain players during particular situations. Schilling used a journal as a workbook and focused on the technical aspects of his sport. At Duke University, *2006 National Basketball Coach of the Year* Gail Goestenkors used journals in a different way. "Each year I ask the players 10 specific questions that they answer in their journal. So the journal . . . is a keepsake for years down the line . . . remembering what their hopes, dreams and desires were" (personal correspondence, June 8, 2006).

My good thoughts are powerful My only negative thoughts are weak! Decide what you want to be, have, do, and think the thoughts of it. Hang on to the thought of what you want. Make it absolutely clear.	Positive thoughts: You will look at balls You will move up You R #1 (No1) GET LOW You are the BEST You will add spin TURN FAST You will have long follow-throughs You will win WIMBLEDON

Figure 7.1 Serena Williams' Musings ("'Serena's No Cheat,'" 2007)

NCAA All-American and PAC-10 diving champion Meg Hostage used an athlete's journal as a teenager. Her club coach required journals for goal setting. "Journaling helped keep us accountable for what we wanted to achieve, and in a way helped us to reach our goals," explained the Stanford University senior. "Putting it all in writing helped remind us what we were working toward every time we opened the journal to make a new entry."

Other athletes use journals to write a full range of motivational, technical, and personal entries. Some athletes draw pictures in their journals; some keep their writing online in a blog with photographs and video clips; others invite coaches, advisors, or thinking partners to read the journal and offer feedback. Again, there's no one right way to journal. Just like Team Notebooks, Athletes' Journals have the potential to open new avenues of learning for both coaches and athletes.

Journal Writing 101

Modes of Writing

Much of the writing found in journals may be identified as "expressive." Of the three modes of writing—transactional, poetic, and expressive—Martin describes expressive as "crucial for trying out and coming to

Three Modes of Writing

Transactional—writing that informs, argues, or persuades like reports, brochures, how-to manuals, summaries, cover letters, resumes, evaluations, Webpages. . . .

Poetic—writing that gives shape to an idea, experience, or observation like adventures, mysteries, poems, songs, plays, or speeches. . . .

Expressive—writing that assists writers in discovering and clarifying ideas or experiences for themselves or for others like journals, memoirs, letters (e.g., sympathy, congratulations), email exchanges, personal reflection, life story. . . .

Adapted from Britton, 1970, 1982; Lightfoot and Martin, 1988; Martin, 1983; Strong, 2001, 2005.

terms with new ideas" (1983). And James Atwater explains that expressive writing enables people to

> make sense for themselves of what they have seen or read or done or talked about by composing it for themselves in their own words. Thus expressive writing is fundamental to learning—in any subject matter—because it enables [writers] to internalize knowledge, to make it part of themselves, by putting it together in their own terms. (1981)

James Britton explains that "[e]xpressive writing is primarily written down speech" (Britton, 1982, 97). It might be overly simplified to say, "Just have your athletes talk on paper," but in a manner of speaking, that's what expressive writing is—with certain differences, as Britton acknowledges.

With talk we have "face-to-face" and "immediate feedback"; with writing, we are "left on [our] own . . . with no [immediate] feedback" (97). Even more, when athletes write a journal entry or compose a notebook page, they may have a tendency to write for the coach, as mentioned earlier in the book. To minimize this influence, provide athletes with opportunities to share their writing with teammates, friends, or parents. A broader audience may just take the athlete's focus off the coach and produce more far-reaching responses.

Writing and Learning

> *"We write about what we don't know about what we know."*
>
> —Grace Paley

Journaling takes us back to Zinsser's *Writing to Learn*. In fact, one of America's foremost writing teachers, Donald Murray, echoes Zinsser when he writes, "We write not to say what we know, but to learn, to discover, to know. Writing is thinking, exploring, finding out" (2005, p. 37). And in the world of athletics, discovery, exploration, and learning help athletes and teams achieve. If you're thinking, "more writing means more learning and that equals more winning . . ." Why not?

The Physiological and Psychological

Journal writing also has the potential to affect an athlete's physical and emotional well-being. For example, athletes who suffer from issues related to stress may struggle in numerous ways, according to the American College of Sports Medicine (Figure 7.2). Coaches and sport psychologists address these issues with athletes through conversation, visualization techniques, Yoga, meditation, and writing. Sport psychologists regularly work with clients from the NFL, MLB, and NHL as well as world-class athletes on National and Olympic teams.

Behavioral	Physical	Psychological
Difficulty sleeping	Feeling ill	Negative self-talk
Lack of focus, overwhelmed	Cold, clammy hands	Inability to concentrate
Consistently performs better in practice/training than in competition	Profuse sweating	Uncontrollable intrusive and negative thoughts or images
Substance abuse	Headaches Increased muscle tension Altered appetite	Self-doubt

Figure 7.2 Selected Signs and Symptoms of Stress in Athletes (American College of Sports Medicine, 2006)

At some universities, sport psychologists provide athletes with writing activities that help sharpen players' mental approaches, curb performance anxiety, and work to eliminate negative talk and thoughts. A sport psychology consultant at the University of Vermont since 1997, Sheila Stawinski developed Performance Feedback, a mental skills sheet for the Catamount athletes (Figure 7.3). "This performance feedback sheet," explains Stawinski, "is an invaluable to tool for assisting athletes in assessing their performances over time, observing negative and positive performance patterns, and helping them determine what mental skills they need to work on to improve their performances."

In Figure 7.3, notice that lacrosse player Danielle O'Dwyer's initial stressor before a match with the University of New Hampshire was the weather, but through "positive talk" as identified in her writing, the athlete attacked the game straight on. Stawinski's mental skills sheet also records a player's level of stress at different times of the competitive day.

Writing assignments like Stawinski's complement Dr. Stephanie Dowrick's work (2009) that identifies the following benefits of journaling:

- reduce stress and anxiety
- increase self-awareness
- sharpen mental skills
- promote genuine psychological insight
- advance creative inspiration and insight
- strengthen coping abilities

We all know athletes who battle stress and anxiety to the point that the pressure negatively affects their performances. What plans could be put in place to help these athletes cope? How does writing a mental skills sheet like Performance Feedback begin to chip away at an athlete's stressors?

Many of us have had to write with a concern to a landlord, colleague, family member, or friend. Perhaps an athletic director has overlooked an issue that has been, in your eyes, vital to you and your team. You've spoken to the AD face to face and left a voicemail with no result. Time passes and your disappointment festers to the level of frustration. Finally, you write an

PERFORMANCE FEEDBACK—UVM

Name: O'Dwyer Opponent: UNH

What were your stressors for today's game? *The weather*

How did you experience the stress? (thoughts, feelings, actions)
Worried the weather would affect the way we play

How was your level of arousal for today's game? *Perfect*

0----------------5/----------------10
Too Low Perfect Too High

What were your feelings at the various times in the day?

Bus ride– *excited*

Warm up– *very excited*

Just before the game– *pumped up*

During the game– *first 15 minutes I worried, but after that I thought we did awesome*

What techniques did you use to manage the stress? How effective were you in controlling it? *Positive talk*

How was your self talk? (Describe) *Good, positive self talk*

What mental training techniques were most helpful to you? *Staying positive*

What did you enjoy about the game? *That we never gave up after being down 6-0*

How would you rate your play? 0----------------5---------/--------10 (*7*)
Poor Average Great

Describe how you felt about today's game?
Awesome. It was a huge win!! Go Cats Go!

Additional Comments? *At first it was a little quiet on defense but once we got our first goal, we completely turned it around.*

Figure 7.3 Performance Feedback Sheet, UVM (Reprinted with permission, Sheila Stawinski, University of Vermont)

email to the AD suggesting that the two of you address the issue with the AD's supervisor, the school principal or college's associate dean.

During the writing process a wide variety of emotions surface. By the end of composing such a letter or email, we may be nervous or anxious but at the same time—because we have addressed the issue head on—we may feel as if a burden has been lifted. In fact, some of us feel liberated. The act of writing has been an emotional release—a catharsis. In their meta-analysis of the research on the benefits of expressive writing, Baikie and Wilhelm (2005) included the following advantages to writing:

- fewer stress-related visits to the doctor
- improved immune-system functioning
- a feeling of greater psychological well-being
- improved sporting performance
- higher grades in the classroom (paraphrased)

These researchers and practitioners, along with learning and writing scholars like Zinsser and Murray, reveal the potential benefits that expressive writing can have on an athlete.

Tips on Journal Writing for Athletes

Some athletes approach a blank page as if heading into the big game. Heads down, eyes zeroed in. Others sit timidly, anxious even, like a 9th grader brought up to sit on the varsity bench. These athletes seize up, stare at the blank page, and can't muster a deep breath. In the world of writing, we hear a lot about the latter response. Some call it *writer's block*; my experience says the writer is thinking too much.

My writing teacher Jared Carter jotted the following quotation on the board during the first day of class:

> *A human being gifted for a particular art attains to a degree of excellence in it exactly in proportion to his ability not to think about it.* –Simone Weil

A French philosopher, Weil died in 1943 at the age of thirty eight. Since that class so many years ago, I've come to think of these words as the forerunner to Nike's catchphrase. Looking back, that's part of what Jared taught us: *just write it*.

Earlier I wrote about a group of ski racers I worked with at Burke Mountain Academy. During that visit, I shared the research and potential benefits of writing. The next day I wrote the young skiers about writing and their ski racing lives. Here's part of that letter:

> *Let's say you commit to writing 3–5 minutes every other day of your training and competitive year (5 minutes × 182 days = 910 minutes/15 hours). And let's say that just a fraction of what these researchers profess will affect your ski racing life. Perhaps your stress will be reduced to some degree; maybe you'll learn more about your technique; or possibly you will enhance your ability to listen and speak with your coach and thereby understand more fully certain facets of race tactics. Would these potential results be worth 3–5 minutes every other day?*

My advice to athletes (or to any writer for that matter) is to put your butt in the chair, your pen to the paper, and make words. Whether we write for 3 minutes or 30, our words have the potential to teach us something. These few tips may also help:

- Don't be overly concerned about the conventions of writing. In other words, don't worry about spelling, grammar, and paragraphing . . . just write.
- Establish a time each day to write. Maybe just before stretching or after a workout. Again, whether it's a three-minute *QuickWrite* or a thirty-minute immersion . . . begin the habit.
- Keep a specific place to journal. Use a journal book, a particular document on the computer, or a blog.
- Draw or sketch. There are many ways to tell the story of your thinking.
- Make a list: One way to jump-start writing is to make a list of thoughts connected to a topic. Then, start writing. Jason Murray, a high school athlete, used this approach on the topic of "losing":

    watching the winners celebrate
    thinking about my mistakes in the game
    coaching decisions?
    facing friends and teachers the next day in school

stupid things people say to me after a loss
MY MOTHER . . . there'll be other days; you'll get them next time,
My father shaking his head—disappointed

I hate watching the winners celebrate after losing a game. I don't care what kind of game it is—pre-season, a pick up game or a championship. It's like the worst thing especially watching the guy I defended go crazy or look over at me with his eyes all squinty and a big stupid grin on his face. If it's after a championship game and we get awards, then we have to wait for the winners to get them. While I'm standing there trying not to look defeated I think about my mistakes . . . .

- Finally, remember Simone Weil.

Kinds of Journal Entries

Generally speaking, there are two types of journal entry formats that athletes tend to use: free writes and guided writing with prompts.

Free Writes

Sometimes athletes pick up their journals and write what's uppermost on their minds. In these "free writes" athletes may focus on an approaching competition, look back at a training cycle, or discuss an issue about a teammate, coach, parent, or friend. In an effort to keep the words flowing, such free-write journal entries can take on a stream-of-consciousness approach. An athlete may begin writing about a coach's decision to taper the athlete's training, for example, and end-up writing a movie review. The purpose of journaling is to unpack ideas—to explore, discover, learn, and know. Remember Donald Murray's words, "Writing is thinking, exploring, finding out" (2005, p. 37). As a result, it does not matter if an athlete weaves and dodges from topic to topic in a journal entry. The ideas are what matters. One kind of free write is called a Quick Write:

Quick Write:

As the name might suggest, a Quick Write has the athlete writing steadily in a short amount of time, usually from 30 seconds up to 5 minutes. This writing approach works well for Team Notebook pages, too, and has benefits that include

- promoting spontaneity and freedom in writing while thinking about practice, training, team, and life;
- supporting critical thinking and focus within the sport;
- encouraging writing as a learning habit for athletes;
- giving athletes time to collect thoughts before speaking to teammates and coaches; that makes this writing activity particularly valuable on teams prior to team talks or with individual athletes prior to a chat with coaches, training partners, and others.

One tip for a Quick Write activity: Whether using a pen, pencil, or keyboard, keep writing. Do not stop! If your thinking gets bogged down, write whatever comes into your head even if it is gibberish—or—write the same word over and over again (e.g., practice, practice, practice). Don't worry, your thoughts and those words will come. They always do.

Guided Writing with Prompts

At times, coaches may assign or athletes may select a "writing prompt." Prompts are statements, questions, or scenarios that trigger an athlete's writing session. These prompts may be personal or technical.

Here's an example by Swedish high school exchange student Jonathan Szeps who played soccer in Michigan. Jonathan wrote in response to the journal prompt "My most humiliating day as an athlete":

> *I easily remember the most humiliating day as an athlete. It was about three years ago when my team had an away game in a suburb called Rinkeby. Rinkeby is one of the suburbs in Sweden with a lot of crimes and problems. It is also a suburb with a majority of immigrants. In my team, almost everybody has their roots in Sweden (I'm one of the few who doesn't). Everybody on the team also comes from pretty wealthy families. A lot of my teammates have a lot of prejudice about Rinkeby. Before the game everybody was joking about how we would get robbed after the game after we easily had defeated the team.*
>
> *When we arrived to the field the win seemed even more obvious. The field was a joke. Not as big as it should have been in our age, not grass, no nets in the goal and the team we were playing didn't even wear the same cloths. We expected an easy victory but we were SO WRONG!*

> *The team, called Benadir, gave us a lesson how to play soccer. On a shitty field in the middle of nowhere they played like the Brazilian national team. They played with us, making cool tricks and scoring beautiful goals. At the end of the first half the score was 10-0 and we couldn't believe what we just had experienced. After some yelling from our coach we got back out for second half. We played a little bit better, scoring two goals (I scored one) but we still got beat by 16-2. After the game, instead of robbing us, the players were really nice to us and behaved like a winner should. We were so embarrassed and all of us didn't say a word on way back home. This really proved us wrong about prejudices. I will never forget that loss.*

Beyond the theme of humiliation in sports, Jonathan's writing reveals one of those life lessons that sports offer. This journal entry could itself be used as a prompt for an athlete's journal.

Quick Write/Prompt:

A three-sport senior athlete headed to Dartmouth, Christian Bennett pens a Quick Write focused on the prompt, "What's a good opponent":

> *A good opponent has class. A good opponent has respect for his teammates, his opponents, his fans, and the officials. He is kind, courteous, does not excessively gloat in victories, or complain in defeats. He is modest and enjoys the sport. Also, I believe it's important that an opponent also remain competitive. If there is no competition, then neither one of you will learn anything from the game, match, or race. Additionally, if your opponent is not competitive with you it will not be enjoyable.*

Quick Write/Snap Shot

A former U.S. Ski Team Coach, Adam Chadbourne carries a notebook and pencil with him to the ski slopes. He uses a Quick Write *Snap Shot* to help his Burke Mountain Academy athletes capture a moment in time. "Whenever there was a breakthrough moment—a great run, one super turn, or what have you—I would immediately hand the notebook and pencil to the athlete, have her put down in her own words what she had just been thinking about in that moment . . . what she was feeling, seeing, what she had done differently. . . ." The page was then torn out of the coach's notebook and returned to the athlete to be transcribed into their personal journals later that day. Chadbourne keeps copies of his athletes' notes for follow-up conversations.

Snap Shots provide Chadbourne's ski racers with opportunities for deeper thinking and work on visualization. Having studied neuroscience in college, the coach explained that "with time, our memory of events will often change dramatically, even within 10–15 minutes. More time equals opportunity for more change."

He goes on to say, "The benefit I see is that this immediate writing in its most raw form is the most true representation of what has occurred. Even [a few minutes later] one's recollection may change. I even ask the student-athlete to pull his or her note out and reread it before the next run even if we discussed [the note] 5 minutes earlier."

A favorite activity among the Burkies, *Snap Shots* add to the ways these athletes think and learn about their competitive performances and training. Those ways can include video review, athlete-to-coach discussions, athlete-to-athlete discussions, journal writing, and group journal writing sessions followed up with discussions. Naturally, the final component of the activity is the athlete's continual reflection on experience.

Journal Prompts

The following list of sample prompts can guide an athlete's thinking. (More prompts may be found in Chapter 8's model journal.)

1. What do you dislike about yourself as an athlete and why?
2. Think back to a time when an athlete or team you admired failed in an event that the athlete or team was favored to win. Describe your feelings.
3. What is your favorite place to compete and why?
4. Why can this statement hold true: "Some days, doing poorly is the most important result that could happen."
5. What is a good opponent?
6. Write about a frustrating experience you've had as an athlete.
7. When is training an absolute joy?
8. Under what circumstances would you allow a competitor to beat you on purpose.
9. What's a great memory that you have as a competitive athlete?
10. What books would you recommend to a young athlete and why?

11. Write about your favorite sports movie.
12. At the present moment what non-athletic jobs look as if they might give you the same "something" that competitive athletics does?
13. Your coach or assistant coach gave you misinformation before big competition . . .
14. What story would you like told or written about one of your teammates or coaches?
15. What story would you like told or written about you as an athlete?
16. Tell the story of a piece of your sports equipment throughout your athletic career (e.g., baseball glove, football cleats, lacrosse stick).
17. Write about an injury that you experienced.
18. How would your life as an athlete change if you had a sponsor who paid you $100,000 per year plus all expenses?
19. Now, a follow-up prompt to #18: What if that sponsor placed the following guidelines on you: If you do not land in the top 10% in all of your competitions in Year 1, your sponsorship will be cut by half ($50,000). In Year 2, if you do not perform in the top 10% in each competition, the sponsorship will by another half ($25,000). By Year 3, if you're not performing consistently in the top 10%, you will be dropped.
20. Write a letter to a person who made a difference in your athletic career back when you were a young athlete.

Writing Activities for an Athlete's Journal

These activities, like some of those suggested for Team Notebooks, help athletes explore their thoughts and feelings and also create opportunities for learning.

An Effective Coach

Sixteen-year-old sophomore Willy Bennett, a bronze medalist in the state wrestling championships, uses a graphic organizer to look more closely at the coaches in his three-sport life (Figure 7.4). Such a writing exercise assists an athlete in recognizing that coaches, like athletes, have both strengths and challenges. The exercise could also provide input to coaches who assign such an activity to their athletes.

A Good Teammate (or Training Partner):

Seventeen-year-old varsity goalkeeper Kyle Gauvin explores the idea of what makes a good teammate (Figure 7.5). As a senior, Kyle will captain his soccer team. Establishing his view of what a teammate should and shouldn't be will help Kyle as a player by identifying his own beliefs; this activity will also help Kyle lead his team. As a full team activity in a Team Notebook, this graphic organizer could prove helpful in priming a full-team discussion about being a good teammate. Kyle, a good teammate himself, has shown us the way.

What Makes an Effective Coach for You?

Characteristics of an Effective Coach ***for you:***

Encourages players	Maintains discipline
Communicates effectively	Tells the truth
Is reliable	Needs enthusiasm
Is proficient in the sport	Knowledge of drills/exercises
(or used to be)	Needs to be able to understand people

Characteristics of an Ineffective Coach ***for you:***

Too strict
Pushes too hard
Does not have firsthand knowledge of the sport.
Does not realize that kids have other commitments.
Does not encourage players.
Is too nice, compliments kids to the point of causing overconfidence

Tell the story of one of your most memorable moments with a coach.

One of my best moments with a coach happened after I placed third in the state for wrestling. Both of our captains were already out, and there was only one other teammate left in the tournament with me. I was telling my coach how I was embarrassed that we did so badly, and that I wanted next year to be better. He turned to me and said: "That's what we need, we need people to care."

Figure 7.4 Identifying the Characteristics of an Effective Coach (Willy Bennett)

What Makes a Good Teammate (or Training Partner) for You?

Characteristics of a Good Teammate (or training partner) for you:

1. Someone that can communicate with you on and off the playing field.
2. Someone that can push you beyond your limits to that next level.
3. A teammate that would rather go to the field to practice their skills than go to a party.
4. Someone that knows how to push their teammates forward through tough times.
5. A teammate that is more interested in seeing you improve rather than him- or herself.
6. A person that is constantly thinking of new ways he or she can help improve the teams performance. With drills or assistance on improving skills.
7. A player that shows up first to practice to work, and stays late after practice to keep working.
8. A player that gets right back into the game if he or she makes a mistake instead of giving up.
9. If a player is hurt, he or she still shows up to practice to help out, shows up at games, to support the team.
10. A teammate that always has your back during tough times outside of the sport.

Characteristics of a poor teammate (or training partner) for you:

1. Someone that gives up or stops training if they are tired and don't want to continue, instead of enduring the fatigue.
2. Someone that doesn't make passes during a game, and tried to do everything himself.
3. A player that shows up late or does not show up at all to practice.
4. A teammate that constantly argues and or talks back to his coaches or captains.
5. Someone that would rather hang out with his or her significant other than show up to practice.
6. Someone that would give up if something bad happened in a game.
7. Someone that wouldn't support his team if he or she got hurt, but instead just gave up on the season.
8. A player that plays dirty in the game and lies about it.
9. A player that pressures his or her teammates into doing something they don't want to do.
10. Someone that does not try in school, and expects to receive good grades from his or her teachers.

Figure 7.5 Identifying the Characteristics of Good Teammate (Kyle Gauvin)

Double-Sided Journal Entry

Good winner	I like playing against teams that know how to win and how to lose. The Cougars have always demonstrated class—they win a lot, and they don't jump all over the place after a victory—they immediately shake hands and talk with the opposition—the players also make sure they speak with the officials and with the opponents' coaching staff. They have class and show it with how they win.
Teammate	A teammate takes care of his own business and prepares well. He comes to practice and games ready to play. A good teammate gives everything on and off the field. He never bad mouths anyone or embarrasses the team. My favorite teammates over the years....

Figure 7.6 Double-sided Journal Entry (Themes)

Double-Entry Journals (Themes):

This writing activity may be used in a Team Notebook or an Athlete's Journal. There are several ways to use a Double Entry Journal (Figure 7.6). The coach may provide sport-specific topic(s) for the left hand-column after a game or during a practice. Or, the coach will provide a list of topics (below) that athletes may choose from throughout the season:

Poor sport	Suck-up	Trainer
Great eye	Focus	Foul
A good loss	Training	Frightened
Natural athlete	Fitness	Technical
Poser	Teammate	Discipline
Future pro	Official	Reward
Injury	Coach	Practice

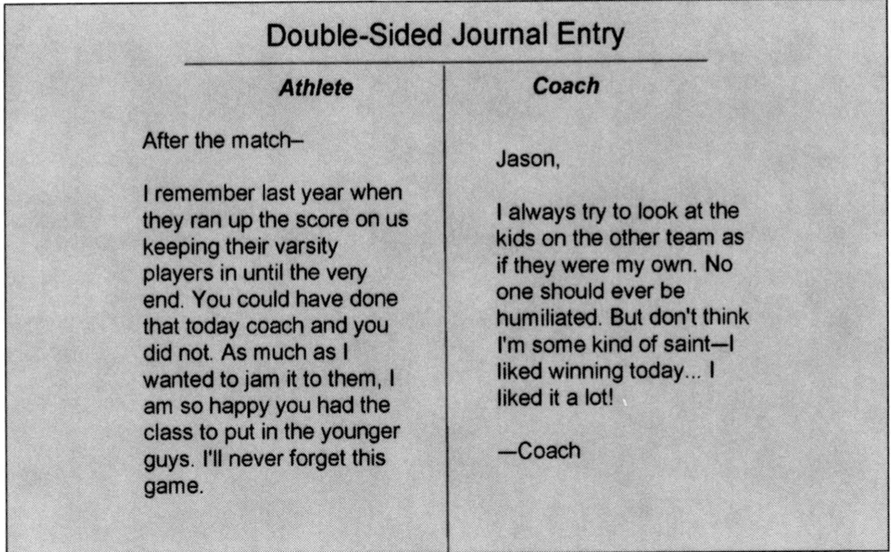

Figure 7.7 Double-sided Journal Entry (athlete to athlete, coach to athlete)

Double-Entry Journals (athlete to athlete, athlete to coach, coach to athlete):

This writing activity may be used in Team Notebooks or an Athlete's Journals. The coach writes an observation or comment to an athlete on one side of the journal page or the athlete writes and the coach responds (Figure 7.7). The same activity can happen between two athletes.

Tag a Teammate:

During this activity athletes will identify teammates who fit certain attributes listed in the chart (Figure 7.8). Athletes will name a teammate and then give examples of their teammate's qualities. As with other activities, coaches may use Tag a Teammate to learn more about individual players much like the sociogram. In addition, depending on the personality of a team, these sheets may be shared in large and small groups as discussion prompts.

This activity may be used to great advantage on travel teams or with teams that have experienced significant turnover in personnel. Ask the athletes to fill out the form identifying teammates from previous teams. In small groups followed by a full-team gathering, athletes will discuss

Tag a Teammate

Who'd make a great coach?	A true sportsman	Dedication plus+	Kindest
Most coachable	Always leaves it on the field	Most motivating	Great future
Great opponent	Team Leader	Fun	Positive
Healthy	Student-Athlete: the complete package	Who should take the last shot	Fitness Fanatic

Figure 7.8 Tag a Teammate

the qualities of former teammates. Such a conversation can help players identify the qualities that matter to them and assist in developing team expectations. In addition, such an activity can remind players that they, too, could be the team's "Kindest" player or be known for exhibiting "Dedication plus." Finally, Tag a Teammate can be one more way to help players get to know one another and as a result build team unity. The activity could be adapted in a variety of ways like "Tag an Opponent," "Tag a Coach," or "Tag a Fan."

Full-Contact Poetry:

Many athletes I know and worked with use poetry to express their understandings and feelings about sport. Some use songs and music. Here are several other approaches to share with athletes about writing poetry for their journals:

Using a List

Ask your athletes to make a list of words that are common in your sport. Then, take those words, play with them, and find creative ways to put them together. Here's an example about football by the team's captain:

FOOTBALL

Floating.
Hard motion.
Bronzed images of old.
A man. A ball.
Explosions of power
Like T.N.T.
Dancing, forgiving.
Coursing moves.
Expecting.
Destinies collide
And live to rise again.
Not for glory
For love.

by Scott Marchildon

Photo Poem

Ask athletes to select a photograph from your sport or provide a collection of photographs. To get the creative juices flowing, try the following:

- Come up with a working or draft title;
- in a 3–5 minute quick write, explain what you see in the photograph or what you might expect to see;
- make a list of sport-specific words (e.g., "home plate"), common phrases (e.g., "Well in!"), or rules from the sport (e.g., "off sides");
- think about who might be telling the story in the poem (the narrator or speaker); and
- think about a character for the poem, and write!

Three-Sentence Poem

Again, using the words, images, actions, and moments of a sport, write a poem using the following template (Wormser and Cappella, 2004):

1st sentence: a setting or action
2nd sentence: question
3rd sentence: an image

Sample Three-Sentence Poem:

Last Play

A stiff breeze,
four quarters of a solid ground game
and an all-conference back
set the play.

Is the fake taken?

Alone in the end zone . . .
the ball spirals true to mark—
he drops it and
wakes to the championship
he lost.

Position Poem

Have athletes write about the position they play in their sport. JT Taylor, my team's sweeper and captain from the late 1990s, wrote about his position as central defender (i.e., sweeper). Here are the first few lines from "Through The Eyes of a Sweeper":

In the distance, leaves rustle on mountaintops.
The bright colors of fall fade with the sun.
Teammates surround me.
We sit, isolated from the commotion;
The field seems miles away.
Here, our minds are clear.
Focused, I stretch, loosening my muscles.
The horn sounds, and the pitch calls my name.

Another way to jump-start your players' thinking could be by passing out some of the best sports poetry. Your local library will have collections such as the following available:

- *American Sports Poems*, R. R. Knudson and May Swenson, editors
- *Motion: American Sports Poems*, Noah Blaustein, editor
- *This Sporting Life: Contemporary American Poems about Sports and Games*, Emilie Buchwald and Ruth Roston, editors
- *Opening Days: Sports Poems*, Lee Bennett Hopkins, editor (grades 3–8)

Naturally, many sports poems may be found on the Web. Assigning your players to find poems or short pieces about your sport could be a great way to fill long bus rides. In fact, why not have a poetry reading in your team hotel or bus. And if you end up having a collection of poems written by your athletes, why not print the poems in a small book and sell the collection as a fundraiser!

Create and Maintain an Athlete's Blog

Many athletes keep online journals and blogs. Some maintain an online presence to keep family, friends, and fans informed. Others write as a way to build and sustain corporate sponsorships. Public journals in the form of blogs or social networking sites motivate athletes because they know that their writing will be read and in some cases responded to. Indeed, as is the case for most writers, having an audience is motivating.

An elite ski racer from northern Maine, Nick Michaud maintains a blog. When faced with a debilitating, long-term health problem, Nick kept on writing in his blog:

> *At the moment, the best Junior [racers] are finishing the last adjustments on their skis. Athletes are running to the start line, finishing up the last of their warm-ups. Coaches are making the last adjustments to skis, and fans and parents are getting ready for a show. But, I'm not there. Months later, having fought an ankle injury, sickness, hives, muscle cramps and something eating away at my body, the struggle that would be the final climb of the course has become as difficult as climbing any stairwell. Why did this happen? How did I get here?*

During his long-term illness, finally diagnosed as a thyroid disorder, Nick worked with a holistic medicine and osteopathic doctor, a neurologist, an Orthopedics and Sports Medicine physician, and a physical therapist. Obviously, writing alone does not help an athlete get well, but writing about his illness may reduce stress, help organize wellness activities, and keep the athlete thinking as an athlete. Nearly a year later, Nick writes,

> *Getting my health under control, my daily activities have shifted from walking up the stairs then immediately needing rest, to sprinting across the [swimming] pool, building muscle in the weight room, bounding, and most recently roller skiing! It feels so nice to have my life back.*

And finally, months later, Nick titles an entry "Re-Sculpting Myself" and writes,

> *I am finally starting to feel like Nick Michaud again. Confident in my abilities, I seem to be my happiest during and after grueling workouts. Without them I feel too average. I am once again reluctant to ski easy when the training plan calls for it, reluctant to rest, and reluctant to finish sessions. I have missed this confidence and joy for training and racing for some time.*

Writing to Health: Injury/Health Report

Along with the blog, Nick kept an Injury/Health Report that chronicled his illness over the course of nearly a year and a half. Such writing is helpful for doctors, coaches, physical therapists—an athlete's entire support team—as they work to restore health. The day-to-day, week-by-week recording does the important work of keeping an athlete like Nick organized when speaking with his support team. In addition, the act of writing keeps Nick involved, is proactive, and can add to his sense of "training" toward health. Here's a glimpse at Nick's report:

> *First 2 Weeks of November 2009 (On-Snow Training Camp: Vuokatti, Finland):* Woke up second morning of skiing barely able to walk. Left Achilles in much pain. Saw trainer from New Zealand who [figured] it may have resulted from something in weight room weeks before. Recovered in roughly 10–12 days.
>
> *Late June:* Met with Dr. ______ who sent referral to get MRI of Cervical, Thoracic, and Lumbar Spine. That morning coach _______ and PT student

> _________ noticed misalignment in hips, chest, neck when lying down; thought they found 3 points where vertebrae out of place when feeling back with hands. During MRI lower back was completely numb, as was left arm; pain in neck and left side of head with tingling in left ear.
>
> July: Met with . . . neurologist . . . who reported significant disk herniation at L5-S1 with loss of lordosis, degenerative disk disease at T7, T8, and loss of lordosis in cervical region. Could not explain upper body. Prescribed 3 weeks in bed using traction during all waking hours.

Diagnosed with a thyroid disorder, Nick wrote to explain,

> My final diagnosis was Bromide Toxicity with Iodine deficiency, low thyroid hormones, and significant disk herniation at L5-S1 with loss of lordosis, degenerative disk disease at T7, T8, and loss of lordosis in cervical region. But the ultimate diagnosis was Bromide Toxicity, as it was a cause (along with training and racing hard through the fatigue and body break down) for the rest of the chain of events . . .

As his last blog detailed, "I am finally starting to feel like Nick Michaud again." Indeed, Nick Michaud is on the ski trail to recovery. And because of expert advice from his support team and his writing, he is also in tune with his body.

Establish and Maintain a Team Social Networking Website

Teams maintain social networking sites and so do coaches and individual athletes. The site keeps family, friends, and fans in contact with each other and can address a wide range of socio-emotional-athletic realities with potential benefits to the writer (and reader).

Some of my former players started a Facebook site for our 3rd- to 5th-grade soccer club. These former players, now parents, serve as volunteer coaches for their children's teams. I do not think any of the 9- to 12-year-olds participated on the Facebook site directly, but their parents/guardians, older siblings, former club players, friends, fans, and coaches got involved to share pictures, cheer on players, trade information about match sites and times, and learn more about the rules of the game. We also used the site as a place to highlight the achievements of former players, so the current youngsters could get a sense of the program's history and their connection to it.

Athlete←→Thinking Partner

In both formal and informal ways many of us serve as a thinking partners to our athletes and coaching colleagues. A thinking partner listens and asks questions to help another explore ideas and issues. A thinking partner does not tell someone what to do—it's about coaching and guiding . . . or what most of us consider effective teaching and mentoring.

These days, most of my work as a thinking partner occurs in email exchanges with athletes and coaches. Such a back-and-forth promotes exploratory writing and broader thinking, and therefore enhances learning. Serving as a thinking partner has its benefits, too. When I write back, I think about my own thinking . . . and I learn.

Should coaches set up their athletes with thinking partners? I think a lot of us do this as a matter of course. At the end of my high school coaching career, I began assigning senior varsity athletes to incoming 8th-grade players. The two swapped email and on occasion met for pizza. I'm sure the varsity athlete answered questions about classes and teachers at the high school. But the relationship served a greater purpose; it provided the young student-athlete a connection to the high school during that critical middle school–high school juncture. In some cases the partnership turned into a big brother relationship that lasted through the season.

Many of us at the high school level connect our 11th- and 12th-grade players to former players who have moved on to the college ranks. The same happens when college players move to the next level. Such connections are vital; the back-and-forth conversations create opportunities for the younger athlete to sound off and receive feedback.

And so . . .

Writing in journals provides countless opportunities for athletes to explore their thinking and address emotions. Journals are also a great place to learn. The following chapter provides one example of an Athlete's Journal.

Chapter Eight

Athlete's Journal: Creating a Template

Some athletes just need paper and pen—writing is simply a part of how they negotiate the world. But other athletes—perhaps the majority—will benefit from being given an Athlete's Journal that's similar to the Team Notebook. Here's how to create one.

Creating a Template

For coaches who work with individual athletes like runners or tennis players, creating a practical Athlete's Journal will involve merging knowledge of the sport, the athlete, and writing-to-learn activities. Here are topics to consider when developing a basic journal:

Purpose: The Athlete's Journal will complement the coach's teaching, focus on issues such as training, learning, and competing, and encourage the athlete to explore areas such as motivation, visualization, and goal setting.

Frequency: How often will the athlete write? Some athletes are energetic writers. They keep blogs, diaries, and Facebook pages, and they also text and Twitter. Others, not so much. Discuss the benefits of writing with individual athletes and then together agree on a middle ground of how often the athlete will write. The template introduced in this chapter has a 10k-road racer writing entries twice a week.

Choice: An Athlete's Journal is a part of how a coach teaches an athlete. In effect, writing is a part of training and practice. However, since writing can be personal, even intimate, a well-received Athlete's Journal provides opportunities for the athlete to be in charge and have choice. A coach may want to allow prompts to be substituted or, in the case where a journal will be shared with a coach, permit athletes to label an entry "Please do not read" or to take the entry out of the notebook all together. Ultimately, the most effective journals for athletes are those that they feel in charge of.

Prompts: Make a list of critical pieces of information that an athlete may want to address in an Athlete's Journal. Look back through this book for prompts, templates, quotations, activities, and graphic organizers for ways to introduce these critical pieces of information. If you're designing a journal for one specific athlete, emphasize areas that the athlete might benefit from addressing. Be flexible and willing to revise your plan after introducing the journal to your athlete.

Digital Options: An athlete may be accustomed to writing online in a blog or on Facebook—or at the very least, feel more comfortable writing on the computer. The athlete may wish to continue using digital media like blogs because they provide an audience and that can be motivational. Discuss issues of confidentiality and encourage the athlete to share more personal writing through email.

Privacy: Parent/guardians of under-age athletes should be informed of their child's journal. Although the journal is private personal writing, if a coach reads writing that may suggest an issue (e.g., an eating disorder), the parent/guardian will be informed. Underage athletes should be aware that their coaches have an obligation for the athlete's safety first and foremost.

Swift River Runners, An Athlete's Journal

This Athlete's Journal has the following components:

Cover Page: personalized with athlete's name, team or club, and quotations from stars of the sport.

Coach's Letter: an introductory letter then highlights features of the journal and offers advice about writing.
Prompts: thirty different prompts for a 15-week season.

Free-Choice Journal Prompt Suggestions
Blogs: suggested blogs for runners.
Quotations on Running: running stars and others offer their words. These quotations may be used for free-choice prompts.

There are a number of ways to create or adapt the Athlete's Journal. Try adding components of the Team Notebook or including the athlete's Training Log as a part of the journal. There's no one right way. As with Team Notebooks, create a journal that works for your athlete and you.

Cover Page

Athlete's Journal

Morgan Caroline Trevett
Swift River Runners

"Your body will tell you what to do."
–Joan Benoit Samuelson
1984 Olympic Gold Medalist, Marathon

"Spend at least some of your training time, and other parts of your day, concentrating on what you are doing in training and visualizing your success."
–Grete Waitz
New York City Marathon, 9x winner

"To get to the finish line, you'll have to try lots of different paths."
–Amby Burfoot
1968 Boston Marathon, Winner; Journalist

Swift River Runners

Dear Athletes,

Welcome to the Swift River Runners!

For some, our running club has become a second family. For our newcomers . . . *Welcome!* We wish you a successful season. Maybe you'll set a PR. Perhaps you'll make the top ten or land on the podium. No matter what your accomplishments, remember, it's always about "the run."

As you know from our preseason meeting, we ask that you keep your Training Log up to date with your actual training numbers. We will review the log with you every other week to make sure the program we designed with you fits your needs. We also ask that you keep this Athlete's Journal—yes, it's your runner's homework! We believe that if you take time to write and reflect that you'll learn a lot more about your running and yourself. Write two entries per week on Tuesdays and Thursdays—more if you'd like. Plan on about taking 8–12 minutes per journal entry. A few prompts will take longer like when you watch a *YouTube* video or read and write about a chapter from this year's SRR book, *Runner's World Guide to Road Racing*. Here are some tips for your journal writing:

Don't be concerned with perfect writing. In other words, don't stop to check spelling, correct grammar, or create perfect paragraphs . . . *just write*. Think about the journal as a fun cross-training day.

Establish a time to write, like after you stretch.

Many athletes keep their journals in their runner's kit. If your journal is close by, you may end up writing more than two entries a week. We think that's a good thing! Extra writing prompts may be found at the back of your journal.

Draw or sketch. There are many ways to tell the story of your thinking and your running . . .

If you're struggling with a particular journal topic, make a list of words that connect to the topic. Once you have a list of 8–10 words, start writing about each of the words in the list. You'll be amazed how your thoughts flow.

Run with your words and enjoy . . . .

Yours in Running,

Coach Kiesman Coach Waite Coach Broomhall
Coach Adams Coach Morgan

Journal 1 **_Tuesday, May 8_**

Journal Prompt: *Time Line: Draw and label a time line of your athletic career thus far. Identify your athletic milestones, coaches, significant changes. . . .* (See the Time Line model at back of journal.)

Journal 2 **_Thursday, May 10_**

Journal Prompt: *Write about some of your athletic favorites. Why are they your favorites?*

Elite runner	*Training partner*	*Place to run*
Place to compete	*Opponent*	*Shoes*

Journal 3 **_Tuesday, May 15_**

Journal Prompt: *Three-Minute QuickWrite:* What makes training hard for you?

Journal 3 Back page:
Journal Prompt: *Three-Minute QuickWrite:* What makes training easy for you?

Journal 4 **_Thursday, May 17_**

Journal Prompt: *Write a 10k road race:* tell the story of one of your 10k races. Begin with your pre-race routine all the way through your cool down. Remember to write about the nitty-gritty like what you ate, how long you warmed up, pre-race visualization, thoughts at different stages of the race, pacing strategy, the effect of other runners on your race, recovery . . .

Journal 5 **_Tuesday, May 22_**

Journal Prompt: Read and highlight the 10k section in Runner's World Guide to Road Racing: After reading and highlighting areas of interest, make a list of points of interest and select at least three of them to write more about in relation to your own training.

Journal 6 ***Thursday, May 24***

Journal Prompt: *Athlete's Choice:* Select a prompt from the list at the back of your journal.

Journal 7 ***Tuesday, May 29***

Journal Prompt: *Letter to former coach*: Write a letter to one of your favorite former coaches. You may wish to include the following:

- what you're doing now as an athlete
- the coach's contributions to your career
- the issues you currently face as an athlete
- a fun memory from your time with this coach
- a picture from "back in the day," if you have one
- personal news beyond sport

Journal 8 ***Thursday, May 31***

Journal Prompt: *Effective Coaching:* Write about what makes an effective coach *for you?*

Characteristics of an effective coach for you:
Characteristics of an ineffective coach for you:
Tell the story of one of your most memorable moments with a coach:

Journal 9 ***Tuesday, June 5***

Journal Prompt: *Compose a Three-Sentence Poem.* Use the words, images, actions, and moments of a sport, write a poem using the following template:

1st sentence: a setting or action
2nd sentence: question
3rd sentence: an image

Model:

Here's a three-sentence poem written by Charlie Bloomfield:

He pushes out of the gate,
The cold, frigid air forgotten,

The sound of the earth disappears
And it's a race.

"How was your run?"

"I did it—I stayed
ahead of it and attacked,
but I fell at the end and through the finish"—
but victory isn't a fast time.

Journal 10 — *Thursday, June 7*

Journal Prompt: *Keep the following Calendar for the week.*

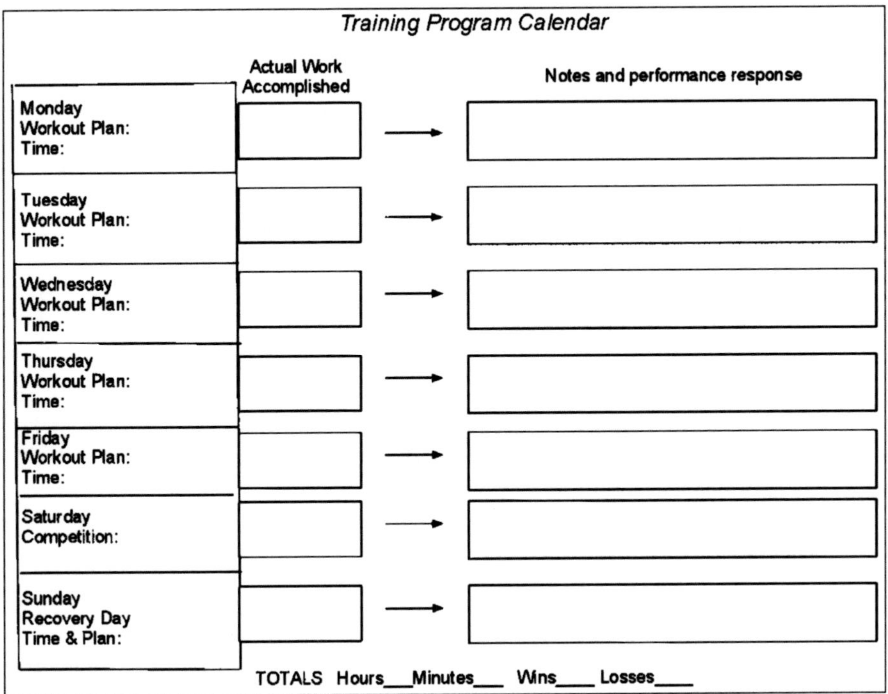

Training Program Calendar

	Actual Work Accomplished		Notes and performance response
Monday Workout Plan: Time:		→	
Tuesday Workout Plan: Time:		→	
Wednesday Workout Plan: Time:		→	
Thursday Workout Plan: Time:		→	
Friday Workout Plan: Time:		→	
Saturday Competition:		→	
Sunday Recovery Day Time & Plan:		→	

TOTALS Hours___Minutes___ Wins___ Losses___

Journal 11 — *Tuesday, June 12*

Journal Prompt: *How do you like the calendar so far?* After 2 days, how does this calendar compare to your Training Log? Does it work for you? Should we think about adapting your Training Log? Come back to this prompt on Sunday to see if you have any more thoughts.

Journal 12 **_Thursday, June 14_**

Journal Prompt: *Five weeks into the competitive season, and here's how I feel about each of the following. . . .*

Training	*Competitions*	*Coaching*	*Rest*
Nutrition	*Life beyond sport*	*The next 5 weeks*	

Journal 13 **_Tuesday, June 19_**

Journal Prompt: *Draw a picture of "the moment" so far in the season:*

Journal 14 **_Thursday, June 21_**

Journal Prompt: *At this point in the season, I can tell I'll need to work on _____________ for next competitive year. Explain what you need to work on and how you might accomplish the work.*

Journal 15 **_Tuesday, June 26_**

Journal Prompt: *Make a list of words that identify your running season so far. Put those words in an online Word Cloud program. To change up this activity, ask fellow runners and coaches for words, too.*

Journal 16 **_Thursday, June 28_**

Journal Prompt: *Trade journals with a fellow athlete. Ask them to write on a subject of interest to them within your sport. Once you get the journal back, write a response.*

Journal 17 **_Tuesday, July 3_**

Journal Prompt: *Watch a YouTube video on the 10k run and write about the following prompts:*

- Title of Video and website address:
- New information you learned:
- Questions you had after watching the videos:
- Ideas you might share with a fellow runner:
- Knowledge you might share with a coach:

- Suggestions you'd make for revising the videos:
- Why the club should or should not watch the video:

Journal 18 **Thursday, July 5**

Journal Prompt: *Write a note, letter, or Facebook message to one of your opponents.* You do not have to send this note.

Journal 19 **Tuesday, July 10**

Journal Prompt: *Watch a competition on YouTube or a sports channel . . . write about it.*

Journal 20 **Thursday, July 12**

Journal Prompt: *Good training partner. List and explain the characteristics of a good training partner:*

Journal 21 **Tuesday, July 17**

Journal Prompt: *Athlete's Choice:* Select a prompt from the list at the back of your journal.

Journal 22 **Thursday, July 19**

Journal Prompt: *Write a letter to a teammate, past or present.*

Journal 23 **Tuesday, July 24**

Journal Prompt: *Food Journal: Keep track of everything you eat on either a practice day or a competition day. Show the journal to your coach and discuss.*

Journal 24 **Thursday, July 26**

Journal Prompt: *You've met a less-experienced runner. They ask you the following questions—what's your advice?*

- When should I replace my running shoes?
- When is it OK to run through pain?
- Should I eat before a run or road race?

- On a rainy day is it better to run outside or on a treadmill?
- What if I have to take a break from training?
- How can I avoid stopping for bathroom breaks during runs?

Journal 25 ***Tuesday, July 31***

Journal Prompt: *Quotation:* Write about the following quotation or select a journal prompt from the back:

> "Champions aren't made in the gyms. Champions are made from something they have deep inside them—a desire, a dream, a vision."
>
> —Muhammad Ali

Journal 26 ***Thursday, August 2***

Journal Prompt: *Critique the following 8-week training plan that prepares an intermediate runner to go for a PR (personal record) in a 10k race (Luff, 2011).* Write about the program's strengths. What might you change in this program? How does this program differ from the one you follow?

Week	Monday	Tuesday	Wednesday	Thursday	Friday	Saturday	Sunday
1	CT or Rest	4 x 400 IW	3 m run	:30 tempo	Rest	4 m run	:30 EZ
2	CT or Rest	5 x 400 IW	3.5 m run	:35 tempo	Rest	5 m run	:35 EZ
3	CT or Rest	6 x 400 IW	3.5 m run	:35 tempo	Rest	6 m run	:35 EZ
4	CT or Rest	7 x 400 IW	4 m run	:40 tempo	Rest	6 m run	:40 EZ
5	CT or Rest	8 x 400 IW	4.5 m run	:40 tempo	Rest	7 m run	:40 EZ
6	CT or Rest	8 x 400 IW	4.5 m run	:40 tempo	Rest	7.5 m run	:45 EZ
7	CT or Rest	6 x 400 IW	4 m run	:40 tempo	Rest	8 m run	:45 EZ
8	CT or Rest	3 m run	:40 tempo	3 m run	Rest	Rest	10K Race!

Tempo Run = easy to near race-pace to cool down
CT = Cross Training IW = Interval Workout

Journal 27 ***Tuesday, August 7***

Journal Prompt: *Write about the largest road race you have run in. Remember the crowd, the opponents, your result, your thoughts, what you learned from the experience . . .*

Journal 28 ***Thursday, August 9***

Journal Prompt: *Start planning the next road-racing season.*

Journal 29 ***Tuesday, August 14***

Journal Prompt: *Write a letter to an athlete who will be joining our club next year . . . or free-choice journal*

Journal 30 ***Thursday, August 16***

Journal Prompt: *Come up with as many statistics as possible about your racing season—they may be serious and not so serious. Write comments about some of them.*

How many training hours?

How many races?

Race times.

Great moments.

Disappointing moments?

Number of miles traveled to competitions?

How many hours run?

How many miles run?

How many race T-shirts collected? If you have a favorite, describe it or sketch it and tell why it's your favorite.

Journal 31 ☺ ***Tuesday, August 21***

Journal Prompt: *"Dear Swift River Runners Coaches . . ."*

Prompts for Free-Choice Journal Entries

Write for 8–12 minutes on a prompt that interests you. Change the prompts in any way you'd like. Please recommend other journal prompts to the coaches.

1. What is something you do well as an athlete?
2. Write a letter to a young runner who is beginning to show promise.
3. What disappoints you about some opponents?
4. What's the most frustrating experience you've had as an athlete?
5. What's your best memory while competing?

6. Other than winning a competition, what's your proudest moment as an athlete?
7. Other than a coach, a partner (e.g., husband, wife), or close friend, who brings out the best in you as an athlete and why?
8. Describe a day when training felt like drowning.
9. You just tweaked a muscle, sprained an ankle, or know you're coming down with an illness—what's that like?
10. Describe an obnoxious fan.
11. Describe an official who was an absolute disappointment.
12. Describe an athlete you would never want to be a teammate with.
13. What words inspire you prior to an important competition?
14. Describe your lucky . . . (e.g., socks, equipment, hat, pre-competition meal).
15. What do you consider unlucky?
16. Describe a special day for you as an athlete.
17. During a long training session, what do you think about? Try to map out your thoughts during that training session.
18. Where do you see yourself as an athlete in the next 3 to 5 years? How do you get there? Why do you need to do to accomplish these goals.
19. When did you know you had what it takes to be a *good* athlete in your sport?
20. Describe your earliest memory as an athlete?
21. When you were young, whom did you admire as an athlete and why?
22. Whom do you now admire as an athlete and why?
23. If you were your coach, what one piece of advice would you offer? (This prompt is a tough one: be objective!)
24. Describe what it's like to hit "the wall."
25. Think about an athlete you know well. Offer one piece of advice that will move that person to a new level.
26. Have you ever been dishonest or cheated as an athlete? If so, why?
27. What's your worst memory while competing?
28. Make a musical play list for training and explain your song selections.

29. Tell the story of your most humiliating day as an athlete.
30. What words do you least like to hear before an important competition?
31. Describe a day or time period when you were closest to giving up as an athlete.
32. Tell about a time when you were genuinely happy for another athlete's success or performance.
33. What is your least favorite place to compete and why?
34. Have you ever witnessed someone cheating as an athlete? Tell the story.
35. If you could relive one moment as an athlete, what would it be and why would you want to go back?
36. Draw a picture of yourself after a loss.
37. Draw victory.
38. Looking back over the years as an athlete, if you could have a "do-over" what would it be?
39. Write about an athlete who is a "poser."
40. During my athletic career, I couldn't stop laughing when . . .
41. If I were not competing in my sport, I would be . . .
42. Write a letter to a person who made a difference in your athletic career back when you were a young athlete. Think about mailing this letter. . . .
43. Write a letter of advice to your young athletic self.
44. After my days as an athlete, I plan to . . .
45. Look back at the results of the last competition you won or did well in. Think about the losing team or look at the name and time of the last-place finisher. What if that athlete were you . . .
46. What have you saved from your youngest days as an athlete and why? (e.g., a newspaper clipping, a piece of equipment, a trophy)
47. Why does this statement hold true: "Once in a while, you have to be willing to accept a poor training day." Do you have an example?
48. During my athletic career, I came close to tears or cried when . . .
49. Write about the kindest thing you have ever done as an athlete.
50. Write about the movies of your athletic life. Is there that one movie—or several—that motivates or inspires?

51. What three nonathletic jobs, careers, or experiences at the present moment look as if they might give you the same special "something" that competitive athletics do?
52. Why does this statement hold true: "Some days, doing poorly in a race or competition is the most important result that could happen." Do you have an example?
53. Write a letter to someone who has suggested that you stop your involvement in athletics and "get on with your life."
54. Tell the story of when your body really let you down as an athlete.
55. Write from the perspective of your youngest competitive self about the athlete you have become.
56. Write a conversation between you and an incredibly gifted young athlete who is not living up to her or his potential.
57. Remember back when you were a young athlete—write about the athlete that you have become from your young self's perspective.
58. Tell the story of when your mind really let you down as an athlete.
59. Come up with five T-shirt sayings about your competing or training. Here are six to jump-start your thinking:
    Got $V0^2$ Max?
    Train Here, Train Now
    Max Out.
    Live at the Threshold.
    Yeah, training.
    Go train yourself.
60. Write about the following quotation:
    "In life, I have but one simple desire: To tear down the sky."
    Alberto Tomba, Italian Ski Race
61. Write about the following credo:
62. "It is more important to participate than to win."
    The Olympic Credo
63. Complete a "Making Meaning" exercise on a topic of your choice:

Topic: ______________________

Possible topics: coaches, training, equipment, race day, focus, cross-training, mental strength, dedication

Step one: Using single words name some of what [Your Topic] is to you. Place those words on the left-hand side of the chart below.

Step two: Name the opposite of those words to create a dialectic. This is important because reconciling (i.e., merging) opposites or reasoning contrary arguments helps us arrive at the truth (i.e., there are always two sides to everything):

Step three: Place some of the opposing words in a true sentence about your subject:

Step four: In the final step, we use strict form to help us make meaning. Write one paragraph of five sentences about [Your Topic] using the following guidelines:

Sentence 1	a five-word statement
Sentence 2	a question
Sentence 3	two independent clauses combined by a semicolon
Sentence 4	a sentence with an introductory phrase
Sentence 5	a two-word statement

Runners' Blogs:

Keep your eye on various blogs maintained by or for runners. Just use your favorite search engine to find various sites. Blogs can offer great advice in some cases, like

Emilie Manhart's *One Mom in Maine*, scrumptious recipes: www.onemominmaine.com/

Scott Dunlap's A Trail Runner's Blog: www.RunTrails.blogspot.com/

Marathoner Ryan Hall's blog (http://ryanhall.competitor.com/)

Visit USA Track and Field for more blogs (http://www.usatf.org)

Quotations on Running

Endless lists of quotations by runners and athletes may be found within books, online lists, and articles. Often, such quotations make for good writing prompts for your journal or are just fun and inspiring to read:

> "There will be days you don't think you can run a marathon. There will be a lifetime of knowing you have."
>
> *–Unknown*

> "Some people create with words, or with music, or with a brush and paints. I like to make something beautiful when I run. I like to make people stop and say, 'I've never seen anyone run like that before.' It's more than a race—it's a style. It's doing something better than anyone else. It's being creative."
>
> *–Steve Prefontaine*

> "The body does not want you to do this. As you run, it tells you to stop but the mind must be strong. You always go too far for your body. You must handle the pain with strategy . . . It is not age; it is not diet. It is the will to succeed."
>
> *–Jacqueline Gareau*
> 1980 Boston Marathon champ

> "Running has given me the courage to start, the determination to keep trying, and the childlike spirit to have fun along the way. Run often and run long, but never outrun your joy of running."
>
> *– Julie Isphording, Marathon winner*

> "The long run is what puts the tiger in the cat."
>
> *–Bill Squires*

> "Do or do not. There is no try."
>
> *–Yoda*

> "I always loved running . . . it was something you could do by yourself, and under your own power. You could go in any direction, fast or slow as you wanted, fighting the wind if you felt like it, seeking out new sights just on the strength of your feet and the courage of your lungs." *~Jesse Owens*

–End of Journal–

Themes of an Athlete's Journal

Most athletes will want their journals to have a variety of themes. For the Swift River Runner's Journal, at least eight different themes kept the athlete turning the pages. Those themes included training, sport-specific teaching & learning, creating community, reflection, creative journal entries (e.g., drawing, poetry), athlete's love of sport, planning & goal setting, and athlete's history. As you prepare an Athlete's Journal, label each journal entry with a general theme just to make sure you're including enough variety.

And so . . .

Journal writing adds a new dimension to an individual athlete's training while enhancing communication and amplifying learning. For athletes like Serena Williams journal writing can be motivational; for the Curt Schillings of the athletic world, journal writing serves the technical side of sport. And as you'll read in the next chapter, for world-class athletes like David Chamberlain, journals may be used to enhance training, ponder decisions, and earn podiums.

Chapter Nine

David's Story: Writing toward the Podium

"I like free writing . . . it's a meditation, trying to open up the mind and go for it."

David Chamberlain

David Chamberlain began cross-country skiing at the age of 5 in the foothills of western Maine. At age 7, he began racing. Like the parents of countless young athletes, the Chamberlains shuttled their son throughout New England from one ski race to another. A blonde-haired wisp of a boy, David fused superb technique with a titanic engine. Even back then, people knew that David had the tools to go far.

And he did. By the age of 31 in the midst of his ski-racing prime, David boasted a résumé that placed him among the world's elite skiers. A two-time NCAA All-American, two-time North American SuperTour Champion, and three-time World Championship competitor with the U.S. Ski Team, David raced across our planet's snow belt. Sponsored by sports companies and the Maine Winter Sports Center, David worked as a full-time athlete with his sights set on the Winter Olympic Games.

World-class cross-country ski racers train year-round and use April as a recovery month. Known for their cardiovascular fitness, Nordic skiing athletes compete in two techniques: classic (looks like running on skis) and freestyle (looks like ice skating on skis). Races range in distance from sprints of 1 kilometer (.6 of a mile) to marathons of 50 kilometers (30 miles). "Physiological testing shows cross-country skiers to be some of the fittest athletes in the world. The Norwegian champion Bjorn Daehlie, for example, has the highest oxygen uptake of any athlete ever tested" (Nash and Loomis, 2000). And when ESPN gathered a panel of experts to rank sixty sports for their degree of difficulty, Nordic skiing landed among the four toughest in the distance endurance sports along with rowing, cycling, track & field distance events (ESPN, 2011).

To complement and inform his life as an athlete, David wrote in a journal and training log. He kept blogs for Maine Winter Sports Center and FasterSkier.com, an online ski-racing magazine. He also exchanged email and letters with coaches and advisors (e.g., physical therapists, doctors, ski technicians). In the following section David's writing and his insights reveal the role writing can play in an elite athlete's career.

David's Writing

After graduating from Bates College, David settled into life as a full-time athlete at the age of 22. Ten years later, at the height of his career, he trained 850 hours a year and constantly packed and unpacked his equipment to travel throughout the world (Figure 9.1).

Even without the big-money endorsements of prime-time professional athletes, David's life would pique almost anyone's wanderlust—training in a Norwegian indoor ski tunnel, racing in Europe in front of thousands of passionate fans, and skiing the early snow at Yellowstone. David's athletic life focused on training and competing, traveling and eating. In a journal entry on the first training day of the year, David reveals one constant challenge: finding the capacity to fully rest on recovery days (Figure 9.2).

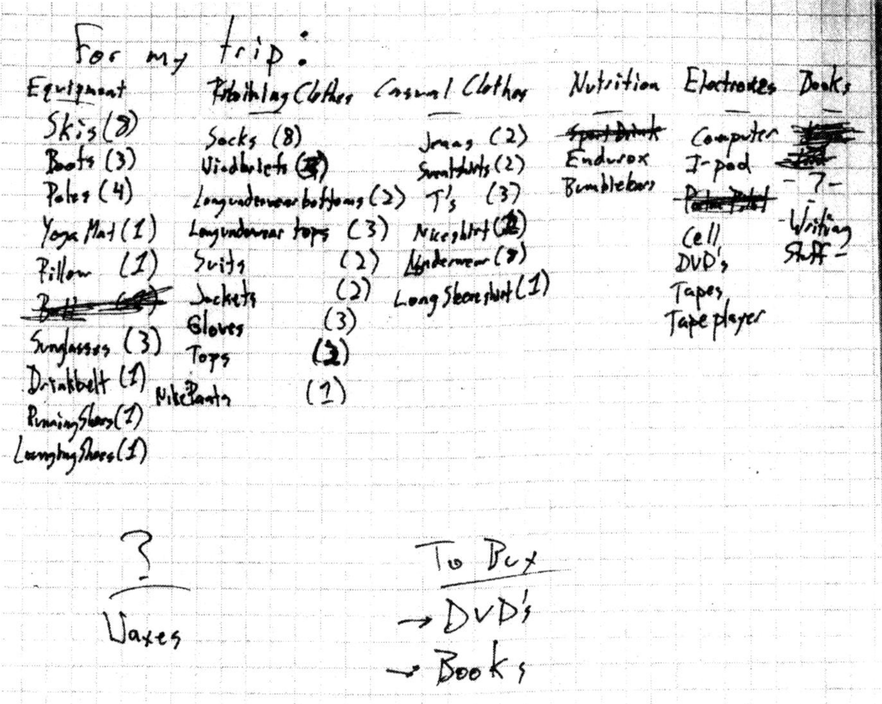

Figure 9.1 Packing List for Europe

David's journal entry could serve as an engaging prompt for young athletes to read and write about.

Looking at the variety of writing that David undertakes throughout a year reveals the different ways his words provide support and complement his athletic and personal lives. Among the most important writing activities any athlete undertakes are training plans and training logs.

Training Plan and Training Log

A training plan is an athlete's road map for the year; a training log is a record of that yearlong journey. Often designed in 3-week training cycles that build upon one another, an effective training plan for a Nordic skiing athlete guides the racer toward peaking at the most significant races of the season. In David's case, World Cup events and

05/01/06

The first day of training for 06/07! I am doing something a little different this year. The first day of training is going to be a recovery day. Something that I have noticed over the years is that I have absolutely no trouble motivating myself for hard training days. It is the rest days that I need motivation for. Rest days are for staying inside and putting up the feet with a good book. And not only that, they are for emotional rest. The athlete that is good at simply doing nothing and validating that activity is the athlete that has a training edge. The spaces that are carved out in the day to do nothing are the times that real recovery takes place. That means putting aside the stack of bills, turning off the phone, closing the email program, and tune out all the mental conversations that happen inside the head. The most important thing is being able to push aside the nagging feeling that no "progress" is being made while I am wrapped up in my covers watching Groundhog Day on DVD. Although any good sport scientist will tell you that is *when the progress is made.*

Figure 9.2 Journal Entry "Rest days"

the U.S. National Championship week often stand out as the critical competition periods.

A training plan is not a monolith. Such plans may be tweaked and revised according to an athlete's performance in training and competition. Moreover, if David is injured or laid low with an illness, his training plan is adapted. At the end of each day, David records his actual training numbers, activities, and notes in his training log.

Figure 9.3 shows David's training log for the first week of the 2006–2007 training and competitive year. Notice that the exercise times are listed in the different training levels. These training levels are based on David's heart rate (e.g., L1 = Level 1, working heart range of 120 to 145 beats per minute; L2, Level 2, working heart range of 130 to 155 beats per minute). In the right-hand column of the training log, David writes notes at the end of each day to record what he did for exercise, how he felt ("F–legs tight" = Feeling–legs tight), and who he worked with. To further capture the effectiveness of a training day, David uses the symbols + (good), 0 (normal), – (not good). It's interesting to note as he explained during an interview that he continually adapted his training log throughout his career:

	Time			Methods					Levels				Comments
Week #18	**Session 1**	**Session 2**	**Total**	**Run**	**Ski classic**	**Ski free**	**Run Sp.**	**Bike**	**L1**	**L2**	**L3**	**+/o/-**	
Mon		1:30	1:30					1:30	1:30			o	AM-off PM-L1 bike ride with team
Tues	2:00	1:00	3:00				2:00	1:00	2:30		:30	o	AM–pole running L3 intervals w/speed warm down PM–recovery bike ride on rollers
Wed	1:30	1:15	2:45		1:30			1:15	2:45			+	AM-RC with DP PM-recovery ride on rollers
Thurs		1:50	1:50					1:50	1:50			o	AM-off PM-easy long bike
Fri	1:00	1:30	2:30	2:30					2:30			-	AM-easy run with BethAnn PM-run with Will and group. F- legs tight and tired, moving into the house today
Sat	1:15	1:00	2:15	1:45			:30		1:45		:30	O	AM-treadmill test PM-recovery run with BethAnn
Sun		2:45	2:45					2:45	2:45			+	AM-off PM-easy long bike F-long week this week, moving a lot, driving back and forth to close on house
TOTAL	**5:45**	**10:50**	**16:35**	**4:15**	**1:30**	**0:00**	**2:30**	**8:20**	**15:20**	**0:00**	**1:00**		

Month of May Comments:

Not feeling good about the last two weeks of the month. Not enough hours, we'll see. Trying to move and finish up at Gould and settle our summer plans has taken a toll on training. My hope is everything will settle for a good June, July, and August. When all was said and done, I had too many hours, oops, not by much and some of the hours that I counted in there were very easy recovery yoga sessions. So I hit the nail right on the head with training hours.

Figure 9.3 David's Training Log, May 1–7, 2006.

> *Every year I change how I keep my training log. I might do it on the computer or I might have a little notebook . . . or a three-ring binder—I don't think I have had two years in a row where I've done the same thing. I don't know why that is, but I think I am always looking for a different way, something that works. I don't quite know why I haven't found it; each way is fine, but . . . I think part of it might be that each year, it is nice to have a fresh start. It's like buying a new notebook, you know.*
>
> (Personal interview, April 17, 2006)

Both the training numbers and the words in David's log provide him with the necessary information to assess the ongoing season and, at the end of that season, to plan for the next.

Making Meaning, a Writing Activity

To help David think more about his Training Plan, I led him through a writing activity called "Making Meaning" (Kent, 2000, pp. 41–43). This activity helps athletes unpack and make sense of issues like training, coaches, or losses that they may face; such activities can also frontload team or athlete–coach discussions. Notice how this activity builds to a statement about training plans that helps David express his thinking:

Making Meaning of Your Training Plan

Step one: Using single words name some of what a training plan is to you. Place those words on the left-hand side of your paper.

Structure
Guide
Order
Log
Challenge
Future
Results
Rigid
Overwhelming
Cumbersome

Step two: Name the opposite of those words to create a dialectic. This is important because reconciling (i.e., merging) opposites or reasoning contrary arguments helps us arrive at the truth (i.e., there are always two sides to everything):

Structure . . . . *chaos*
Guide . . . . *lost*
Order . . . . *disarray*
Log . . . . *unrecorded*
Challenge . . . . *easy*
Future . . . . *past*
Results . . . . *content*
Rigid . . . . *flexible*
Overwhelming . . . . *simple*
Cumbersome . . . . *light*

Step three: Place some of the opposing words in a true sentence about training plans:

If I do not have my training plan as a ***guide*** *I feel* ***lost.***
I would like to enjoy the ***content*** *of the training plan as well as the* ***results*** *it can give me.*
A training plan should feel ***light*** *rather than* ***cumbersome.***

Step four: In the final step, we use strict form to help us make meaning. Write one paragraph of five sentences about your training program using the following guidelines:

Sentence 1, a five-word statement
Sentence 2, a question
Sentence 3, two independent clauses combined by a semi-colon
Sentence 4, a sentence with an introductory phrase
Sentence 5, a two-word statement

Training plans are sometimes stifling. When do they become this? On the days my body feels good the training plan seems fine; on days when my body feels bad I am scared that the training plan is too much for me. In July and November and sometimes the end of January, these are the months that I feel this the most. Must change.

–July 27, 2006, Pineland Farms

Making Meaning focused David's attention by identifying the issues he faces with his training plans. That kind of organized thought can only help him as he designs his next training plan.

Of the writing David accomplishes during his year, journals address both the day-to-day issues and the larger career-centered concerns.

Reading David's journals creates a vibrant picture of one elite athlete's journey—his accomplishments, disappointments, and demons.

Journals

Some athletes write daily journals as if these entries are simply one more training activity to check off during a training day. As for David, he wrote daily training log entries, but when it came to his journal, he explained, "Sometimes two weeks go by and I don't write anything. Sometimes two weeks go by and I write something every day. It's more [about] curiosity . . . why am I feeling this way?"

Those "whys" continually surface in his writing. "All those other things that happen outside of the training session, those are probably equally important as what I've done during training . . ." like if he's had a real stressful week. He goes on to explain that "There are certain things that just kind of throw you off" and these topics often motivate this athlete's journal writing.

In a 570-day period, David wrote 300 entries. Those entries were as short as a few words and as extensive as multi-paged entries with hundreds of words and sketches. Generally speaking, David's journal entries can be categorized as either personal or technical. Looking at the themes of his entries, as well as how often he writes about those themes, presents an idea of this athlete's physical and emotional needs as well as the benefits journals might provide.

Themes: What Does a World-Class Athlete Write About?

In David's case, just about anything. . . . Throughout his handwritten journal books and typed entries, a reader finds David's menu for a game-day football party and drawings of Yoga poses and stretches (Figure 9.4). Readers would not be surprised to see journal entries that focus on heart rate and health (Figure 9.5).

There's also an experiment in seeking balance suggested by a massage therapist. David called the experimentation "The Left Hand Project." Figure 9.6 shows a small section of the entry. The central paragraph of the journal reads,

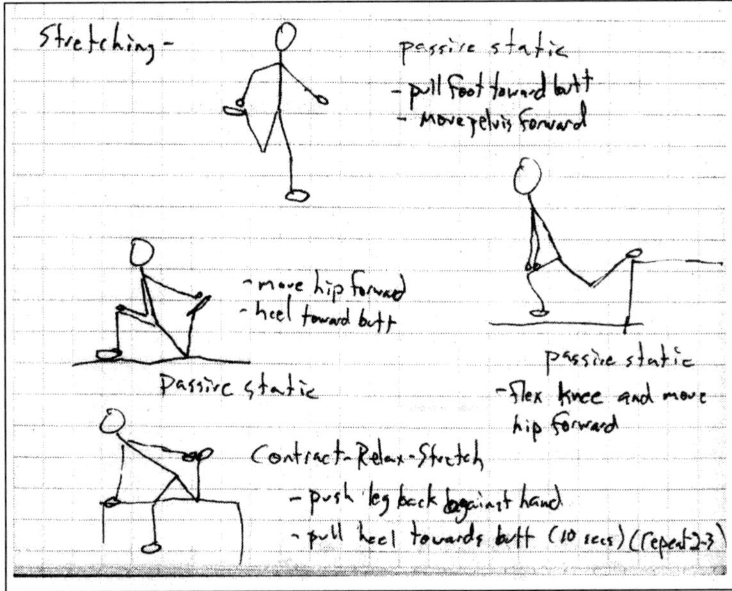

Figure 9.4 Journal Entry "Yoga poses and stretches"

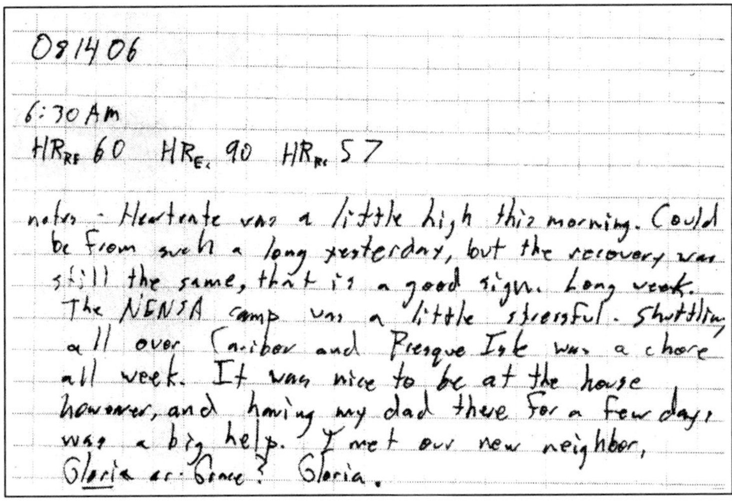

081406

6:30 AM

HR_{RE} 60 HR_{EX} 90 HR_{RE} 57

notes - Heartrate was a little high this morning. Could be from such a long yesterday, but the recovery was still the same, that is a good sign. Long week. The NENSA camp was a little stressful. Shuttling all over Caribou and Presque Isle was a chore all week. It was nice to be at the house however, and having my dad there for a few days was a big help. I met our new neighbor, Gloria or Grace? Gloria.

Figure 9.5 Journal Entry "Heart-rate"

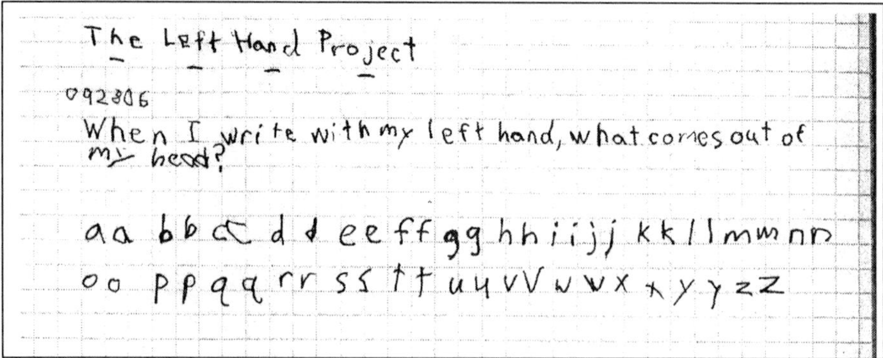

Figure 9.6 Journal Entry "The Left Hand Project"

> *When I write with my left hand, what comes out of my head? The left hand project means only to write with my left hand all the time I am working on the left hand project. To write with my left hand may allow me to work on producing better alignment in my body. I have also heard that sometimes it allows the mind to open up a little [more] to address parts of me that remain hidden. Plus, it looks cool, like I am six years old again.* 092806

Twenty-eight central themes emerged in a year and a half of David's journals (Figure 9.7). The most commonly addressed themes reveal a balance between his personal life and his athletic life.

Naturally, some journal entries included multiple themes; in addition, certain major themes incorporated a series of subthemes. When David wrote about his emotions, for example, he also wrote about meditation and Tarot card readings.

What seems central in all of this is that David is thinking and writing about issues that matter to him as a professional athlete and as a person. He writes about corporate sponsorships and his training, being a husband and a friend. Here are two examples from David's journal. One is a *personal* journal entry and the second is an *athletic* journal entry.

To Ski or Not, a Personal Journal

Near the end of the 2006–2007 competitive year, David writes fourteen pages of journal entries over a four-day period about whether to keep

Personal Journal Themes	**Athletic Journal Themes**
Loneliness . . . 18 entries	Training Sessions . . . 15 entries
Family . . . 13 entries	Focus . . . 13 entries
Emotional Self . . . 12 entries	Physical Conditioning . . . 13 entries

Journal Themes and Frequency of Entries

Loneliness . . . 18	Understanding the human body . . . 10
Training sessions . . . 15	Writing . . . 9
Family and friends . . . 13	Bettering oneself . . . 8
Focus . . . 13	Need for accomplishment . . . 8
Physical conditioning . . . 13	Self-esteem, playfulness . . . 8
Emotional self . . . 12	Schedules and lists . . . 8
Food . . . 12	Equipment and company sponsors . . . 8
Dreams . . . 11	Balance, alignment, and symmetry . . . 7
Body tension . . . 10	Asserting oneself . . . 7
Colors and visualization . . . 10	Need for fulfillment and satisfaction . . . 7
Awareness of body and mind . . . 10	Optimism, personal goals, and self-encouragement . . . 6
Relaxation and breathing . . . 10	Questioning career and life plan . . . 6
Preparation, control, routine . . . 10	Frustration with training or body . . . 3
Yoga . . . 10	The world (environment, economy) . . . 3

Figure 9.7 Themes and Frequency of Entries for David's Journals

ski racing or not. He's 32 years old, has nearly 200-sanctioned ski races to his credit, and has an offer to coach and teach at a well-regarded independent school. In his first entry on the topic, David organizes his decision making in a step-by-step process. Next, he thinks through his future plans by posing central questions (Figure 9.8).

Like many of us during decision-making times, David creates a side-by-side comparison in Figure 9.9 as part of his process. Notice how the theme of "giving up" pervades the opening lines on both sides of the comparison. It's also interesting to see how David creates a foundational statement near the bottom of the journal that reveals other peoples' influence on him.

On day four, David devotes an entire page to a sketch showing where he stands with his decision making (Figure 9.10). David looks to be in a deep hole.

*What is it I am trying to accomplish with skiing?

Where do I even start? There is so much there, so many emotional trails,
I have no clue which one to start on first? Why do I want to give up on the
path I have chosen?

Do I feel that paths are closing in on me?

Yes (money, money, money)

Do I feel that I truly desire to go in a different direction?

No

Do I feel that I don't have the energy for another season?

Yes, but that can change quickly.

Do I feel helpless in finding the energy for another season,
how do I do this?

Yes

Do I feel that I actually have no clue what I am
doing with anything?

Yes

Why have I been a skier, why do I want to be a skier?

I really don't know.

Is all this on a body level, the feeling that my body is pooping out on me?

Could be.

If I had everything I wanted in skiing, results, security, money to be a skier, the thrill of the big competitions, along with it the emotions of being at the top, the lights (Actually, what I really want is the feeling that me and my body actually belong there, with all that goes along with it.), the suits, the crowds, the cameras, would I simple rest on those laurels when I was done and not seek out new challenges? I am trying to put my finger on something here, and I can't do it. Maybe these emotional trails as I called them all lead back to the same place? Where is that and how do I get there?

Figure 9.8 Journal Entry March 8, 2007

Also on day four, David writes a full page free-write on his decision, and then he identifies the central features of his decision making by writing the following:

- Healing
- Pro's and Con's of each direction
- Competition + Jealousy
- He wants something

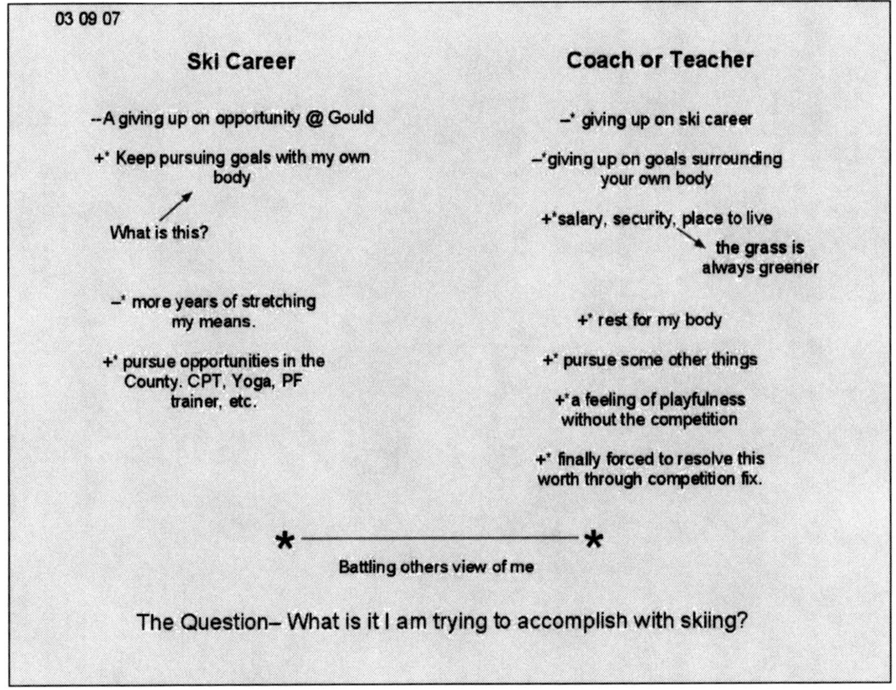

Figure 9.9 Ski Career v. Coach or Teacher

Ultimately, David makes his decision in his third March 12th entry:

> *How did I put it? Mostly this decision is about whether or not I want to continue skiing at the same level that I have been. If I had been given this scenario 2 or 3 years from now, I would have jumped at the chance to run the ski program. But I do not have the sense of completion with my ski career, I don't know if I am dealing with*

It's interesting that David ends his 14th and final entry with an incomplete sentence that trails off, as if, in a small way, he continues the debate. But after 5 days of thinking and writing—and discussions with important others—his decision is made: David continues ski racing for another 3 years.

Writing the Previous Season, an Athletic Journal

As he completes one athletic year and begins planning the next, David reviews the data he has collected in his training logs, race results,

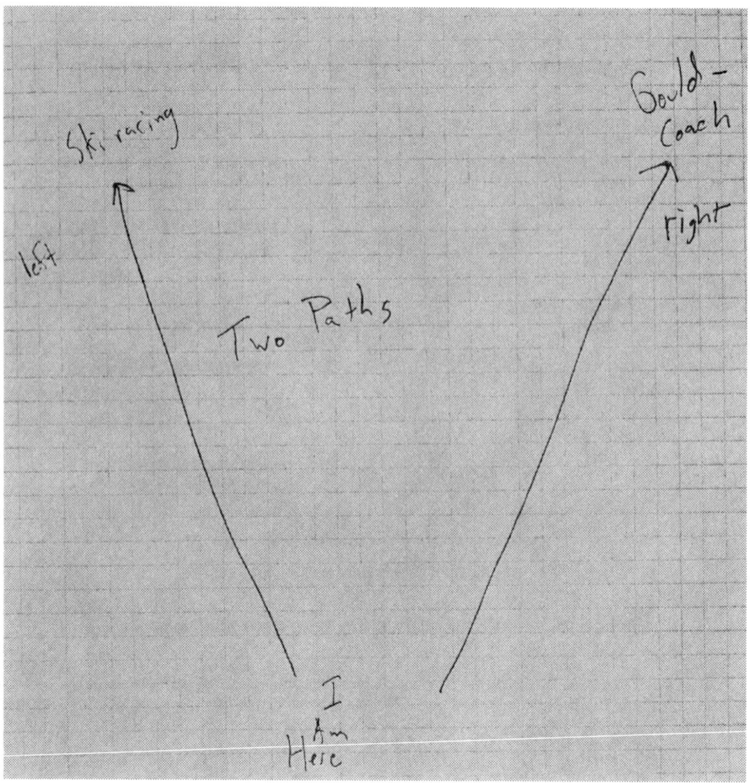

Figure 9.10 Journal Entry "I am here."

journals, notes, and blogs. Then, he summarizes the year in a journal entry (Figure 9.11) and debriefs his initial thinking and new training plan with coaches and advisors. Writing this journal reflection helps David think more clearly about the previous year's plan—what worked well and what didn't. This year-end journal entry is like the Team Notebook's Pre- and Postseason Thoughts—providing a place to look back in an effort to make sense of what happened.

He undertakes this planning work during the recovery month of April and explains

> *I look back to go forward. There are all sorts of emotions behind [planning for the next season]—it's exciting, but there is also the element of wondering what to do and if you are doing the right things, thinking about the right things. It is a fun time but it is also a little bit . . . I tread really carefully with where I am looking . . . there is some*

April 2006

Thoughts on training for 2005–2006:

I started in May and early June with about 6 weeks of volume and only L3 workouts where I monitored my lactate very carefully, keeping it at or below 3mmol. I used long distance workouts in the afternoon for recovery and L2 workouts the day after, fitting in strength where I could. I did 2, sometimes 3, intensity workouts a week. This period went very well, I was rested, engaged and having a great time with the training.

Through June, July and the start of August, I did similar weeks to the period above, only every fourth week did a week of L4 and L5 interval sessions, 2-3 interval sessions. The one bump in the road was the last few weeks of July where I felt a bit run down. I backed off the volume a bit, took a few rest days and felt restored by the time I left for Italy in mid-August.

The next phase was an altitude camp in August, early September on Stelvio Pass. I felt great and got some very solid training in. The core of the training was easy volume, with some L3 sessions after the first week of acclimation. With help from the Nor. Biathlon Team staff I was carefully monitoring my intensity level through lactate levels. Despite crashing my roller skis in the last week, this trip was a success.

I took one week very easy with little training after Italy then started up with a 3-week block of intensity. I did 3 sessions of L4 or L5 each week with long distance workouts in between for recovery. I felt very good during this block, but looking back this may have been too much too soon. Two weeks of intensity, less intervals, more L3 in between 4–5, less interval sessions, less hours? These are questions I am asking myself.

October was spent at altitude, a very similar camp to Italy only a little less volume. I was run-down towards the end, this is something that continues to trouble me. I did reasonably high volume for the first week with no interval sessions. The second week there was volume, two L3 workouts and a time trial. The last week I did 2 L3 workouts and some recovery days. This camp ended the summer and fall training.

Through the winter months the focus was racing. Earlier in the winter, when I had a weekend off, I would put in a little more volume and some L4 intensity sessions. During the weeks with races on both weekends, I would do a short, easy L3 session to "repair the threshold". During the two weeks before Nationals I did two L3 sessions, a time trial, and easy training.

Figure 9.11 Journal Entry "Thoughts on training for 2005–2006". (*continued*)

The times when I felt the best were Yellowstone, US Nationals and the Midwest Nor/Am's. The times when I felt the worst were the Alaska races, the World Cups and the race after March 1st.

I got very sick in Europe, the sickest I have been in years, and I am tracing that back to too many races and a poor emotional state in late January, early February. Even with no racing the last few weeks of February, good rest and training, it was too much to overcome and pretty much ruined the rest of season. Spring series was a disaster; I was not feeling my usual self.

The last three weeks I have been taking a rest. Days off, and some short easy bike rides in the sunshine have helped me recover. I am feeling much better and am starting to feel the desire to train come back.

Figure 9.11 Journal Entry "Thoughts on training for 2005–2006". (*continued*)

> *anxiety there for sure. It's what I do; it definitely affects how I perform next season. Sometimes a little thing can make the difference between a great season and one that's less . . . It's an important time.* (Personal interview, April 17, 2006)

David's 2005–2006 race results reveal the effectiveness of his previous year's training. During the year, his most successful race period occurred during January at Yellowstone, in the U.S. Nationals, and in the Midwest Nor/Am Championships. Next to these weeks in his training log he wrote, "Feeling very good." Figure 9.12 shows his race results from January 2006 as recorded on the International Ski Federation website (www.fis-ski.com). As David plans for the next season, he would certainly look closely at the training that led up to these superb performances.

Race date	Place	Nation	Category	Discipline	Position	Points
28-01-2006	Telemark	USA	Nor-Am Cup	10 km C	1	62.98
25-01-2006	Telemark	USA	Nor-Am Cup	SP 1 km C Final	2	
25-01-2006	Telemark	USA	Nor-Am Cup	SP 1 km C Qual	14	153.09
22-01-2006	Mt. Itasca	USA	Nor-Am Cup	10 km C	1	56.71
21-01-2006	Mt. Itasca	USA	Nor-Am Cup	10 km F	3	58.03
10-01-2006	Soldier Hollow, UT	USA	National Championships	2x15 km M Pursuit	4	80.77
08-01-2006	Soldier Hollow, UT	USA	National Championships	10 km F	6	97.40
07-01-2006	Soldier Hollow, UT	USA	National Championships	15 km C	6	75.25
03-01-2006	Soldier Hollow, UT	USA	National Championships	30 km F Msl	5	105.68
18-12-2005	Canmore	CAN	World Cup	6x1.2 km C Team Sprint	21	

Figure 9.12 David Chamberlain's Results in January 2006

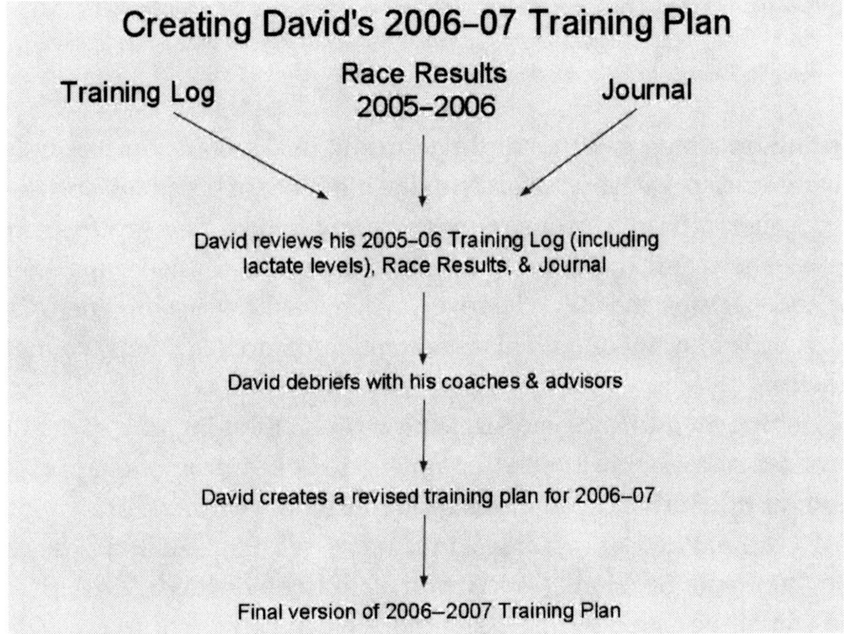

Figure 9.13 The Process of Creating a Training Plan

David's process of designing a training plan is depicted in Figure 9.13. The amount of data he collects and analyzes with his advisors ensures a broad and careful look at the critical pieces of this athlete's year.

Blogs

Keeping blogs helped showcase David's racing life and as a result promoted his corporate sponsors. Beyond the promotional benefits, blog writing provided David with another opportunity to reflect on his athletic and personal life. Such an activity serves as a unique approach for an athlete because he will write with an audience in mind. For David and most of us, adding a readership changes how we writers think and write. In a paragraph of a May 6, 2006, journal entry, David ponders his voice and audience:

> *One question that I always seem to run up against when I write is where does my voice come from? And to whom am I writing? The obvious answer that jumps out is*

> *from me and to me. With a closer look I am not so sure that is the right answer. . . . It would be my goal to have a writing product that is utterly my own voice, but how many influences do I have on this voice?*

Writing on a blog is different than writing in a private journal. In his private journal, David wrestles with the influence of his athletic posse—his coaches, advisors, sponsors, friends, and family. This group shares ideas, beliefs, and suggestions with David and can influence his thinking and decision making. However, when David writes on one of his blogs, he is mindful of both his posse and audience (e.g., fans, younger athletes).

Having an audience can stretch a writers' thinking in a variety of ways and create opportunities for athletes to be self-promotional or self-deprecating. Audience can make an athlete more guarded. For example, David did not debate quitting ski racing on his blog. An audience can also "motivate revision" (MacArthur, & Karchmer-Klein, 2010, p. 57) and sometimes such writing, especially when connected to sponsors, gets sanitized.

And so . . .

Having competed in 258 races on the international circuit, David ended his ski-racing career with 39 podiums and 113 top-ten finishes. Although he did not compete in a Winter Olympic Games, David lived his athletic life without compromise and performed at his highest level. No sponsor, coach, or country could ask for more.

Chapter Ten

FAQs

> "There ain't no answer. There ain't gonna be any answer. There never has been an answer. That's the answer." — Gertrude Stein

Before, during, and after the implementation of Team Notebooks or Athletes' Journals questions will arise. Some of the following questions came from coaching colleagues who either utilize notebooks with their teams or are considering it. As for the responses here . . . as much as I like Gertrude Stein's quotation, there are always answers. However, sometimes those answers vary according to the sport, athletes' ages, and program needs.

I like the idea of Team Notebooks, but I'm maxed out as a coach and not sure I want to add one more thing to my life. What's your best suggestion?
Keep it simple. Try using one or two sections of the notebooks for a season. The Pre-Season Thoughts may be a good first choice. Your athletes will write and you'll read, and this exercise won't take more than 20 minutes for them and 20 minutes for you. Try using the Competition Analysis I sheet for a few games or matches. Or before a team discussion, use a Graphic Organizer to prime your athletes. In all of this, keep in mind that athletics is about learning and the act of writing has benefits.

You may not see those benefits immediately, but for some athletes—and coaches—Team Notebooks will make a profound difference.

Do coaches keep their own Team Notebooks or Journals?
Your choice. Coach Mike Keller of the University of Southern Maine tried out a Competition Analysis I. Here are a few of his responses from a match against Skidmore College:

- My strengths as a coach in today's match:
  Composure—Substitutions—Remaining Positive
- My weaknesses as a coach in today's match:
  Pre-game preparation of the team. Ability to adjust team to 4-3-3. Warm-up players earlier.
- Team strengths in today's match:
  Heart—not giving up—freshmen/first-year players came up big.
- Team weaknesses in today's match:
  Midfield shape, defending holding space, nervousness, readiness to play, communication, leadership

I'm a coach and a master athlete. I like the sound of writing for me. Is journaling the way to go?
Thor Engblom, one of my former ski athletes from the 1980s, is now a serious master athlete. He races bikes and then writes about his racing for family, friends, and himself:

> *In 2002, after a 13-year hiatus, I started cycling again. I had raced in college in the late 80's and even rode across the US. Now, I was in my mid 30's and starting to feel out of shape so I dusted off my old road bike, replaced the tires, tubes, handlebar tape and slid my old touring shoes into the toe clips and headed out for a ride. I told my wife I would not go crazy and buy a new bike or start racing again. It is not a lie if you believe it at the time and, going in, I really had no intention of being where I am now. That is a common thread in all great journeys. And disasters.*

He wrote newsy email and Facebook posts to share his racing exploits. During a twenty four-hour team race on an ultra-muddy track, Thor posted updates to his Facebook site about the conditions, his partner's progress, and his own. I remember writing him something like, "Don't fight the mud—use it." Later, Thor wrote that he thought about my comment throughout the evening hours.

My favorite piece of Thor's writing may be about his first 200-mile road race . . . in Death Valley. DEATH VALLEY? The average 80-degree, October temperatures in the desert were nowhere to be found during this race as the thermometer spiked well beyond the 100-degree mark. Thor and his teammates were knocked out of the race at 106 miles. Nonetheless, he learned and shared his valuable race and training lessons:

> *The Lessons: Learning the Hard Way*
>
> *Strength vs. Distance Training*—when training, I became too focused on putting in long, moderate miles instead of short, tougher miles to get me ready for the climbs. I did not have the strength to keep a decent pace up the long grades so I poured too much energy into the climbs just to maintain a pace. This wiped me out. More strength equals easier climbs for the same speed. Now I use brutal hill work to get ready.
>
> *Heart Rate & Gearing*—I just used standard gearing: 12x25 and a 39x53 and this was ok at the beginning. Soon, I did not have enough gearing and I was anaerobic just keeping enough speed to keep the bike from falling over. In the anaerobic state, you will burn through your stored energy and then: game over. For the really long hilly rides, I now use a compact crank with a 12x27. It allows me to spin as much as I need without ever peaking my heart rate above anaerobic unless I want to.
>
> *Electrolytes & Water*—I found that I needed much more electrolytes than I was taking. I have since doubled the amount that I take and I am also very good about tracking my water intake so I don't start cramping again.
>
> *No Loitering!* — This was the easiest lesson of all: don't stop! At least not for long. It sounds obvious, but on timed rides, the clock is the enemy so you can never stop for more than a couple of minutes before you head off again. We just sat around too long at the stops and this allowed our legs to tighten even more. Now, I fly into a stop, fill the Camelback, do a quick stretch and I leave. I don't even talk to anyone because I don't want to be held up. I'll chat on the bike, but not while I'm standing there.

A year later, Thor put his learning to work in another double century:

> *Epilogue: Success at Last*
>
> September of 2004 I flew out to CA on business and brought my bike. I easily completed the Tour of Two Forests Double Century even though it featured much more climbing (15,500 feet vs. 8,800) and longer hills (30 mile long Pine Mountain climb) by employing what I had learned from Death Valley the year before. I finished 49th of 133 starters in 13hrs and 34 minutes (12hrs, 38 minutes rolling) and I could have easily done another 100 miles I felt so good at the end.

As a former bike racer, I learned from reading Thor's words. Master athletes will experience great satisfaction from writing, and through the process, they will learn and adapt their approaches.

What was the biggest issue or problem you encountered with Team Notebooks?

There were times when players' frustrations came out in their writing. Perhaps they didn't play in a game or, in their eyes, played too little. Entries like the one below might have me questioning whether a player was struggling with playing time and didn't feel comfortable speaking with me:

- My strengths as a player in today's match: *None, I didn't play*
- My weaknesses as a player in today's match: *None, see above*

Then there were also times when I felt a player didn't take the writing seriously enough. Notice the responses below by one of my captains, Ryan Goodwin, after a win:

- My strengths as a player in today's match: *Talking*
- My weaknesses as a player in today's match: *None*
- Team strengths in today's match: *Everything*
- Team weaknesses in today's match: *Corners*
- Opponent's strengths: *Kept it out wide during the second half*
- Opponent's weaknesses: *Not skilled, young*
- What was the "difference" in today's match: *We were awesome*

At first, because he was a captain, I expected a more thorough analysis from Ryan. I kept my mouth shut—and rightfully so. For this match we'd taken a 90-minute bus ride over bumpy roads into the willywacks of central Maine. We played a brilliant match. As our goalkeeper, soon to be named to the all-state team, Ryan captured the entire match *from his perspective* in eighteen words.

Not every entry in a Team Notebook has to be close analysis. And remember: not all of our athletes learn or communicate most effectively through writing—some write what appear to be quick responses like Ryan's and then sit on the bus talking in great depth about the match. Others may phone a teammate, post Facebook comments, text, or Twitter. There's no one right way to make sense of a competition.

Ultimately, I learned to accept my players' writing however they submitted it. The one exception: if I couldn't read it, they had to write it over. Yes, there were times when I'd cringe and times when I'd have a discussion with the player about their thoughts. In about every case, however, those discussions went well. The bottom line: if we don't allow our athletes' writing and their thoughts in whatever form, we're going to receive inauthentic, *please-the-coach* drivel. That writing is not going to help you, the team, or the player.

What was the number one benefit for you as a coach?
Better communication. I got to hear a bit more of players' thinking and their perspectives. As I reviewed Competition Analysis I sheets from the University of Southern Maine, I was struck by the straight talk the twenty-somethings offered Coach Mike Keller. Of course, such honesty is a testament to the relationship Mike has developed with his players. For example, one player admitted that he was "kinda" nervous about playing in a match. Other new players mentioned not totally understanding the system of play that Mike had established. This kind of communication with the coach—not always offered in face-to-face conversations—serves to make the team better.

Coach Matt Grawrock asked the following questions as he began to use Team Notebooks with his National Championship Southern Virginia University Team:

> "I wanted to know if you give the post-season reflection page to the players at the beginning of the season, or at the end? In my situation, I will be trying [Team Notebooks] for the first time, and I wondered if an advance showing will allow the players to get a better idea of what we would want to look at, at the end of the season."

It makes sense to me, as Coach Grawrock suggests, to include all of the Team Notebook pages in the notebook when first passed out. This way athletes have an opportunity to see what's in store for them.

> "Do you have in-season reviews with players where they go over the season so far based on things that come from the notebooks?"

If a coach has periodic meetings with players throughout the season it makes good sense to have the player's Team Notebook available as a reference.

Is it possible to use Team Notebooks or Athletes' Journals with children under 10 years old?
Absolutely. When using Team Notebooks with younger athletes, you may have to modify the wording or eliminate some questions. However, these youngsters do have ideas, questions, and observations that they're desperate to talk about; many of the pages and activities of Team Notebooks offer these youngsters the opportunity to share. As for Athlete's Journals, asking youngsters to respond to journal prompts will help elevate their thinking about the game—that can only help. Furthermore, certain prompts draw out questions that young athletes may not have thought to ask in large group discussions.

Most children begin writing before they enter school and use inventive spelling or drawings to supplement their tangles with more formal language conventions. Letting youngsters "write" about their sports lives will help them explore their understandings of being an athlete and the many issues they will encounter (e.g., being a good teammate, playing fair). Writing and drawing also helps as they learn more about the technical aspects of their sport, from improving skills to understanding tactics. An added bonus: Writing for younger athletes could also complement what's happening at school and at home.

In Chapter 9, a journal entry by David Chamberlain showcased a packing list for a trip to Europe. Five-year-old Carson made a similar list before his first t-ball game of the season (Figure 10.1). The son of a former athlete, Carson reveals his organizational skills and a certain seriousness about his emerging athletic life. For those who may have trouble with a 5-year-old's inventive spelling, Carson's list includes, 2 bats, 3 balls, 1 glove, 2 baseball shoes, and a water bottle.

What about using Team Notebooks or Journals with student-athletes who speak a different language?
English Language Learners (ELL) may struggle mightily with the reading and writing that's involved with Athletic Team Notebooks and Journals. However, this reality doesn't mean they don't have ideas or that they

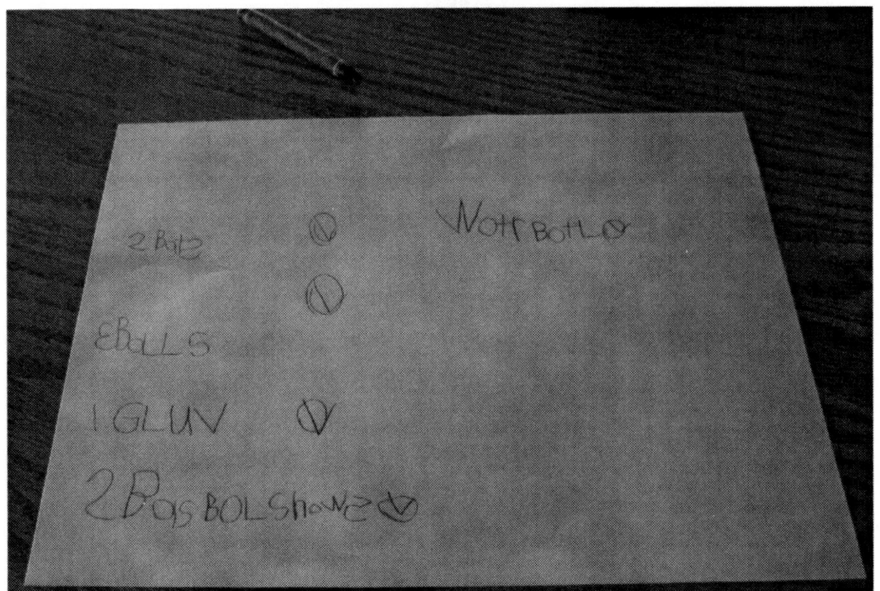

Figure 10.1 Carson's packing list for t-ball

don't want to share those ideas. Indeed, it's not unusual that participation in sport levels the cultural playing field for ELL—an athletic team may be one of the most comfortable arenas in their new lives.

These athletes deserve special consideration and need to hear directly from the coach that whatever and however they write is fine. These athletes' lives, especially if they are newcomers to this country, may have been turned upside down with

- loss of identity, friends, and culture,
- an inability to express ideas or communicate in the community at large,
- high familial expectations for academic success,
- unfamiliar learning environments and teaching styles (*Teaching Today*, n.d.).

The last thing these athletes need is another stressor in the form of the writing that may be required on a team.

Your work with ELL will depend on the athlete's language abilities. You may encourage some players to write responses in their native language. You may not understand the player's writing, but the reality is, this writing is more for the athlete than the coach. You'll find that other athletes write in both English and their native languages. And some will want to do the best they can with English . . . and that means they will have inventive spelling and maybe even some drawings.

You can find support for your English Language Learners from classroom teachers, ELL teachers, writing center tutors, and peer tutors. Many of the athlete's teammates will be willing to help out, too. Pair the athlete with a reading or writing buddy. Together, they may be able to work through any difficulties the athlete encounters. In the end, the writing and discussions that revolve around the notebooks and journals may strengthen your ELL athlete's communication skills because the athlete is writing and reading about a subject that matters.

What issues surface for student-athletes with special needs?

Most of the time school and university coaches are advised about student-athletes who have special needs. Some athletes will have Individual Education Plans (IEP); some will have assistance provided by a 504 Plan. Both secondary school special education programs and the university's academic support services will offer you advice and support. In some cases coaches should talk directly to the athlete to see what can be done to help out. We all learn differently, and our athletes with special needs deserve respect and acceptance.

What can you tell me about the writing that sports psychologists assign to athletes?

All professional teams and some collegiate teams have the support of sport psychologists. Their work involves helping athletes with a wide range of issues such as

Mental preparedness
Managing anxiety
Coping with success
Handling failure
Goal setting
Reward strategies
Visualization
Motivation

Some of the work accomplished with sport psychologists involves writing and some involves discussions, counseling, hypnosis, mental imagery, and so on. Go to your favorite online bookseller, university library, or university program for book suggestions.

I think I have an athlete who would benefit from keeping an Athlete's Journal. I'm not quite sure how to start off the discussion.

In my mind having an athlete write a journal entry is no different than asking an athlete to sit down to talk with you about a race tactic or a wrestling strategy. Writing is just one more coaching tool that helps athletes learn. As a coach you're suggesting the activity because you believe it will help the athlete think more deeply about specific tactics or techniques. Writing can also help the athlete to work on the psychological side of competing. Yes, writing is different from outlining a training program or telling an athlete what to do during a game. It's a teaching and learning tool, but is it so much different from the chalk talk sessions we have in our classrooms or out on the baseball diamond? Well, it is to a certain degree because everyone participates.

Some athletes readily take to journal writing; some don't. If you believe an individual athlete on your team will benefit from writing, why not start out on a trial basis. Explain how professionals, Olympians, NCAA student-athletes, and others write to learn. Let your athlete read David's story in Chapter 9. Next, take the advice from Chapter 8 and organize a journal book for the athlete. Set a goal for so many journal entries per week and see how it goes.

I'm worried that the notebooks or journals might be seen as more homework for my athletes!

Coach Matt Grawrock of Southern Virginia University mentioned this very issue during an interview, saying, "At first the girls seemed to dread having to write. They viewed it as extra homework that they did not like. However, they came to look forward to it, and on some occasions we were not able to hand out the sheets for the notebooks. When we didn't many of the girls asked where they were at and seemed a little upset that they would not have them for the game."

Temple University lacrosse player, Jennifer Homka, echoed Coach Grawrock's words:

> *When we were told that we had to write for lacrosse, we were not too keen about it, because it was our getaway from school. However, when I received the first writing piece I thought it was a great way to express and to think deeply about my experiences and what I need to do for pre-games, games, practices, and post-games thoughts. If I was not given any writing prompts for lacrosse I wouldn't have thought about these ideas . . . writing helped me become a better player and helped me know what I need to do in order to give it 110%.*

I like the idea of keeping a Team Notebook as a coach, and because I enjoy writing, I'd like to add something more. Any suggestions?

Absolutely. After his team's matches, Michigan soccer coach Gavin Richmond wrote Match Ratings for his players. Originally from Newcastle Upon Tyne, England, and an "out of his mind" supporter of Newcastle United, Coach Richmond writes observations of his players and then rates their match performances on a 10-scale:

Match Ratings: Novi Tournament 5/12-13

> ***# 15 Neil***—I enjoy watching your skill and neat control when they come off. I'm not really sure where you think your strongest position is though Neal. Be aware of support players before you receive the ball so you can play quicker. 8/10
>
> ***# 3 Matthew***—A great weekend defensively Matt; you didn't allow anyone to dominate you or push you about. I would still like to see less humping and more passing when you win the ball; it's all about decision making. 9/10
>
> ***# 10 Michael***—I love you playing at full back Mike; you have great energy and speed and like to get forward when you can. Get the ball out of your feet when you look to cross or pass. Trust the left peg! 9/10
>
> ***# 1 Grant***—We are really lucky to have a great keeper behind us Edward. You looked in good form all weekend and your communication is getting better each week. Keep working at your distribution from the floor and out of the hands. 9/10

Coach Richmond also wrote and published one- or two-page Game Reports for players and parents. Here are three paragraphs from one of the coach's Game Reports:

> A grey, murky, wet morning greeted Northstorm 92 as they began the TBAYS Autumn Classic Tournament in Traverse City last weekend. The

> coach felt right at home as the damp conditions reminded him of home back in England. However, the sun rose to brighten up the morning as the first whistle blew.
>
> Ryder L. gave the team the perfect start in their first game against Livonia following up at the back post to slot home. The 2nd half provided more sunshine and more goals as Rico R. added two with clinical finishes. Goalkeeper Grant C., who was let out of his cage, showed some great skill to add a forth near the end. A great start for Northstorm 92 in their hometown tourney.
>
> Flint Arsenal was Northstorm's second opponent of the day and it took a goal from visitors to kick-start the home team into action. A mix up at the back led to a goal for Flint and set up the first comeback of the weekend for Northstorm. Mark M. sneaked into space to finish from six yards out to get the home side on level terms with Rico adding a second soon after. Brady F. finished with a great header from a set piece right from the training ground that delighted the coach and Rico, completing a fine first half comeback with a fourth. The 2nd half saw Northstorm play some free-flowing attacking soccer that had the crowd licking their lips in delight. There was some truly superb footy being played and this was capped when Grant outrageously flicked home a cross between his legs to score the fifth. Neal B. then swiveled in the box to smash home the sixth and complete a fantastic performance. Six-one to the Storm was only half the story.

In Coach Richmond's eyes, writing to his players enhances their learning. "When you write things down and you evaluate and you analyze and you set targets and goals" that's a huge commitment. Richmond, who possesses coaching licenses from both the United Kingdom and America, advises young coaches that writing to players has many advantages. He explained during an interview that writing about players' performances

- showed that he cared about each player and the team,
- revealed that he observes matches carefully,
- helped players understand how he as coach analyzes games,
- proved that he has an eye on each and every player, and
- highlighted the players' and team's strengths and weaknesses.

Interestingly, Gavin hadn't thought about having his players write until he read the *Soccer Journal* articles. His favorite Team Notebook pages were the two analyses because they pushed players to process a game and ultimately become more "accountable."

Richmond's own players spoke highly of the Match Ratings. Goalkeeper Grant Carey explained,

> I always enjoyed the player ratings. I felt that they were a nice way to reflect upon the game. As I remember, they were generally sent out a couple days after each match. Because of this, it was nice to be able to let the emotions (good or bad) about the match settle. This sort of feedback was a good alternative to being reminded about any mistakes directly after a game. [The Player Ratings were] a convenient way to look back on the season and make individual improvements based on your views. (personal correspondence, December 11, 2010)

Interestingly, both Carey and his former coach spoke about the value of the Game Reports for the coach. As Carey explained, "I felt they were more useful for you, as a coach . . . you could record observations and design training sessions based on [the report]." As for Gavin, "Writing game reports helped with how I saw the game. They also showed my players how serious I was about the analysis of matches" (personal interview, December 8, 2010).

My athletes live with cell phones, laptops, and other hand-held devises. Do you have other suggestions for the use of digital media?

Whenever I write about technology, I worry that my words will be obsolete before the manuscript gets into print. In this book I've mentioned the use of social media like Facebook and Twitter as ways to entice athletes to think and write about their training and performances. I've shared blogs by Nick Michaud and David Chamberlain, and suggested having athletes submit their writing online through Blackboard, Moodle, and free-source websites. Here are other ideas, remembering that the technology platform may change but the need to think, share, and seek feedback will remain a constant:

YouTube/Game Summary—as a team activity ask your athletes to share their thinking via video about a game you played or watched, a training session, or an issue in the sport (e.g., High-Tech Swim Suits). The following list may assist with your thinking:

- Athletes could use a Competition Analysis II or a particular journal prompt as the basis for their commentary.

- Athletes could work alone, in pairs, or in units (e.g., offense, defense) to discuss the issue at hand. Perhaps athletes might produce a more creative offering like a sports news commentary. . . .
- Establish a team website, portal, or blog so the YouTube video addresses may be shared. Have a comment section so teammates and others can offer feedback.
- Set ground rules for appropriate commentary (e.g., no criticism of other teams, their coaches, or officials) and length (2–3 minutes).

Twitter, Text, or Facebook/Six-Word Sports Story—as a team activity ask your athletes to write a six-word sports story about a game you have watched together or played in. The six-word format is a popular activity in writing classes and has writers working to create stories in just six words. Many models of six-word stories appear on the Web or in books like *Not Quite What I Was Planning: Six-Word Memoirs by Writers Famous and Obscure* edited by Smith and Fershleiser (2008). A good deal of thinking goes into creating such a story. Here's mine from last night's hockey playoff game: "Into OT— Hail Mary empty netter." Or one on training: "Yearlong training; off-season camps: Made Varsity." The athletes could share their articles on the team's Facebook site or with one another via twitter or text.

Online Newsletter—coach Gavin Richmond's Game Reports and Game Ratings could be included in an online newsletter. The same with the YouTube Game Summaries or six-word sport articles. If the site is open to parent/caregivers, photos could be uploaded to the site. A blog is a good alternative to a full-blown website.

Resource Portal—used for athletes, team personnel, and parents, an online resource portal can be a place to store study guides, practice videos, athletes' blogs and Facebook sites, photo albums. . . . As well as a team's paperwork. My Resource Portal, constructed on the free Portaportal.com site, provides materials for coaches and athletes K–12 as well as parents in our community soccer program. You may access the Resource Portal by going to www.portaportal.com and then typing in *rivervalleysoccer* in Guest Access.

What about writing that gets personal?
One of my student-athletes wrote the following:

It is Christmas. Snow covers
the ground and coats the
trees. The scent of fur bows
fill the air Sled highways
run down the lawn.
Snowmen wave to you as you
drive by. Frozen fingers and
heavy boots. Parades
downtown. Santa Claus and
his reindeer, Rudolf. Cards
in the mail and presents
under the tree. The color red.
Blinking lights on the houses.
Vacation. Wrestling.
Suicide.

After reading this poem, I called Dusty and we met (Kent, 1997, pp. 173–174). Nearly 20 years later he's quite fine. But the truth is, like so many coaches, I have student-athletes who have turned to alcohol, drugs, and other risky behaviors to cope with life's burdens. And yes, some of my kids ended their lives because of these burdens, what must feel like an absolute cavern of hopelessness.

I'm an assistant coach at the collegiate level, and I like the idea of Team Notebooks. What thoughts do you have about selling the notebooks to my head coach?
As an assistant coach at Temple University, Nicole Moore did her homework on Team Notebooks. Coach Moore created a one-page highlight for her head coach, Bonnie Rosen (Figure 10.2), and soon the Owls had their own Team Notebooks underway.

If my principal, athletic director, or a parent questions me on the practice of using writing as a way to learn in sports, what justifications or resources should I provide?
I've never heard of anyone questioning the use of writing as a learning tool with teams or athletes. I suppose, however, there's always a first time. This book will serve as a primary resource. The following

The Advantages for a Team Using the
TEAM NOTEBOOK

For the PLAYER:

- Quick ability to analyze individual play, team play, and opponents
- Ability to see trends in play, actions, thoughts, feelings
- Helps with goal setting and achievement
- Reminder of goals, both team and individual
- Reminder of individual and team strengths, and a reminder of weaknesses (helps with goal setting)
- Way to get feelings and thoughts out in a constructive and useful manner
- Good reference to always turn back to for analysis and understanding
- Ability to take it and run with it. Make it your own tool!
- Opportunities to have coaches know thoughts/feelings—open discussions
- Opportunity to write for oneself.
- Gives insight to teammates and opportunities for team and teammate discussions. Move them to another level.
- Can build confidence, understanding, and motivation for individuals and team
- Ability to think like a coach (analysis of individual, team, opponent)
- Another way to learn about the game of lacrosse

For the COACH:

- Gives insight to coaches
- Opens communication
- Ability to see trends

Most entries will be done on team time

Most questions only ask for short answers. You can write as much as you want, though.

Most entries will take 5–15 minutes

Figure 10.2 Advantages to Using Team Notebooks, Nicole Moore, University of Vermont

resources will also provide sound theoretical reasoning for having athletes write:

Books:

- *Writing to Learn* by William Zinsser (1989, Harper & Row)

"Writing organizes and clarifies our thoughts. Writing is how we think our way into a subject and make it our own. Writing enables us to find out what we know—and what we don't know—about whatever we're trying to learn."

- *Write to Learn* by Donald M. Murray (2005, Thomson & Wadsworth, 8th Edition)

"We write not to say what we know, but to learn, to discover, to know. Writing is thinking, exploring, finding out" (2005, p. 37).

- *Because Writing Matters* by the National Writing Project and Carl Nagin (2006, Jossey-Bass). Though this book does not specifically address athletes and their writing, this volume offers relevant and accessible research on writing. *Because Writing Matters* has a fine chapter about writing to learn (chapter 3, p. 43).

The following Professional Organizations support learning efforts for athletes and coaches:

- *American Sport Education Program*: an education program for athletic coaches
- *The National Federation of State High School Associations*

The following organization espouse writing-to-learn theories:

- *Writing Across the Curriculum*: a long-time organization in the field of writing among American universities. One of the basic principles of WAC is that "writing promotes learning."
- *National Council of Teachers of English*: the primary professional organization for English/Language Arts teachers. One of the organization's statements, *Beliefs About Writing*, reflects the basic principle of Athletic Team Notebooks and Journals:

Beliefs About Writing

Writing is a Tool for Thinking

> "When writers actually write, they think of things that they did not have in mind before they began writing. The act of writing generates ideas. This is different from the way we often think of writers—as getting ideas fixed in their heads before they write them down. The notion that writing is a medium for thought is important in several ways. It suggests a number of important uses for writing: to solve problems, to identify issues, to construct questions, to reconsider something one had already figured out, to try out a half-baked idea. This insight that writing is a tool for thinking helps us to understand the process of drafting and revision as one of exploration and discovery, and is nothing like transcribing from pre-recorded tape. The writing process is not one of simply fixing up the mistakes in an early draft, but of finding more and more wrinkles and implications in what one is talking about" (National Council of Teachers of English "Beliefs About Writing"). *http://www.ncte.org/positions/statements/writingbeliefs*

I've read about Writing Across the Curriculum and Writing Across the Disciplines. I'm wondering whether entire sports programs have used notebooks or journals?

After my first articles appeared in *Soccer Journal*, a number of coaches and school administrators contacted me about instituting Athletic Team Notebooks and Journals across all sports in their school's athletic programs. Three urban school administrators from New York City—a principal and two athletic administrators (both coaches)—spoke about the benefit writing in athletics might have with English Language Learner student-athletes and young people who struggle in classroom.

Burke Mountain Academy weaves writing through its athletic programs and classrooms. I'm amazed at how writing is at the core of so much that happens at this exceptional school. To read more about BMA's efforts, visit their website (www.burkemtnacademy.org/) and read "Reflection at the Age of Speed" by Tom DeCarlo, Academic Director (News & Views Newsletter, Fall 2010).

Writing to learn in sport is an emerging area of research. I'd encourage coaches and administrators who adopt Athletic Team Notebooks and Journals to share their stories in journals of sport and education. There's a lot to be learned from all of us.

Anything else?

THE LONDON SCHOOL OF ECONOMICS AND POLITICAL SCIENCE

CARR-SAUNDERS HALL OF RESIDENCE

18–24 Fitzroy Street, London W1P 5AE, Tel: 01-580 6338/9

22nd April 1988

Mr. Kent ,
UK Connection
Room 130

Dear Mr. Kent,

We have received a number of complaints from residents about noise at night, running along corridors, and even playing football. It seems to be from members of your group.

Can you please ensure on this your last evening here students behave in a quiet and orderly manner.

We hope you have enjoyed your visit to London and your stay at Carr Saunders.

Yours sincerely,

The London School of Economics and Political Science is incorporated in England as a company limited by guarantee under the Companies Acts (Reg. No. 70527) Registered Office as above.

Yet another example of how writing helps with learning.

***

And so . . .

If you have questions or would be willing to share your experiences and ideas about writing to learn with athletes, please visit my website (www.writingathletes.com).

Conclusion

Just Write It.

While on tour in England, I took the teams to visit the requisite tourist traps in greater London. Each year, we visited Sir Christopher Wren's architectural wonder, St. Paul's Cathedral. It's the perfect place in London to bring American teenagers on tour. Not only does this 300-year-old cathedral, replete with clattering walkways, lay claim to one of the largest domes in the world, but also the 528 steps to the tiptop serve as a fitness challenge. From the Golden Gallery visitors may look down at a harrowing, free-fall view from about 280 feet while standing on a small glass window in the floor. At St. Paul's, the Maine kids got adventure, culture, and exercise in one fell swoop.

After racing up the first 257 steps of St. Paul's, the young athletes swarm into the Whispering Gallery at the base of the humungous dome. Here, the boys read about the gallery's irresistible quirk: a whisper against its wall is audible all the way around to the opposite side. (Imagine the odd challenge that this feature presents to teenagers.) The view from high up in the Whispering Gallery reveals an opulence of gold-leafed artwork and architectural perfection.

On one trip, our fun-loving goalkeeper stood in the Whispering Gallery alongside Jerry Kiesman, my friend and long-time colleague. More accustomed to farmlands and dense pine forests than such extravagance, Steve grew oddly quiet as he leaned on the banister and took in the cathedral's magnificence. His mouth agape, he stared at the huge dome above . . . and then he turned to Jerry. Next, he looked down to the Cathedral's floor and surveyed the statues of royals, artists, and statesmen—he gazed at the stained glass windows and chandeliers . . . then, he turned back to Jerry. Finally, this young man from Wilton, Maine (Population: 4,123), leaned out over the railing, bowed his head, and in a moment, glanced back up, whispering, "Kinda makes you wanna spit, don't it?"

Some players end their St. Paul's visit with a silent prayer in an adjoining chapel. Others shimmy through the crowded gift shop searching for just the right present to take back for mom or that special someone. A number of boys cruise the cathedral's parking lot seeking *Paradise*: a tour bus filled with Swedish girls. And a few corner a cathedral guide to talk more about the history of this elegant house of worship.

Our teams comprise a variety of unique characters with distinctive personalities. They learn, communicate, and process information in different ways. Even on the field of play they reveal their differences: Some athletes love to score points while others live to stop them. Bring a team to one of the world's most amazing cathedrals, and well, we just never know. Our athletes make coaching a challenge, a learning experience, and, often, a very good time.

And so . . .

If the idea of instituting writing on a regular basis is overwhelming, don't do it. Tryout an activity, an abbreviated version of the Team Notebook, or, if you want to use a Journal with an athlete, start with one or two writing prompts a week. My nephew Ryan plays water polo at Stanford University. The Cardinals don't write regularly. "Occasionally in our team meetings," explained Ryan, "our coach passes out paper and asks us to write about our thought process during certain game situations . . . counter attack defense sticks out in my mind as one we have done multiple times." The coach reads several out loud as a front-loading activity to a team discussion. According to Ryan, the process helps with team tactics and visualization.

And back at Gonzaga University, Amy Edwards offers sound advice to fellow coaches. "Make sure you value the information you are collecting," she said. "If the players do not feel you value their words then they will be very hesitant or resistant to putting much effort into it. Writing is a great tool for communicating with your athletes and provides a segue to ask questions, to get suggestions from players, to recognize trends . . . . "

As for me, I am picturing my high school team after a night match. It's 9 p.m. and we're stretching in the middle of the field. As the players finish their cool-downs, they pull out their notebooks and begin writing. Some kids scribble quickly and finish in a minute or two; others spend a bit more time. Something is happening during those few minutes of reflection, and I know it helps my players and our team.

You'll be surprised at how your athletes dig deep with their writing, as if they're in the midst of a critical game. They'll examine their play, think about the next training session or game, and write in ways that may surprise you both. And when you stop for dinner after a game, while some of your athletes are piling into a corner booth—others, you'll discover, will be back out in the parking lot, head down, writing on the bus.

References

American College of Sports Medicine. (2006). Psychological issues related to injury in athletes and the team physician: a consensus statement. (2006). *Official Journal of the American College of Sports Medicine*, Retrieved from http://www.acsm.org/AM/Template.cfm?Section=Clinicians1&Template=/CM/ContentDisplay.cfm&ContentID=6273

Atwater, James. 1981. "Better Testing, Better Writing." A Report to the Ford Foundation.

Baikie, K.A., & Wilhelm, K. (2005). Emotional and physical health benefits of expressive writing. *Advances in Psychiatric Treatment, 11*. Retrieved from http://apt.rcpsych.org/cgi/content/full/11/5/338

Britton, J. (1970). *Language and Learning*. Harmondsworth: Penguin.

Britton, J. (1982). *Prospect and Retrospect: Selected Essays of James Britton* (Ed. G.Pradl). London: Heinemann.

Cheville, J. (2001). *Minding the Body: What Student Athletes Know About Learning.* Portsmouth, NH: Boynton/Cook.

DeCarlo, T. (2010). "Reflection at the Age of Speed." *News & Views Newsletter, Fall 2010.* East Burke, VT: Burke Mountain Academy.

Dowrick, S. (2009). *Creative Journal Writing: The Art and Heart of Reflection*. New York, NY: Tarcher/Penguin.

ESPN. (2011). Boxing's knock-out punch. (n.d.). *ESPN Page 2*, Retrieved from http://sports.espn.go.com/espn/page2/sportSkills

Ferrance, E. (2000). *Action Research*. Providence, RI: Northeast and Islands Regional

Educational Laboratory at Brown University.

Gardner, H. (1983). *Frames of Mind: The Theory of Multiple Intelligences.* New York: Basic Books.

Gardner, H. (1993). *Multiple Intelligences: The Theory in Practice.* New York: Basic Books.

Kent, R. (1997). *Room 109: The Promise of a Portfolio Classroom.* Portsmouth, NH: Heinemann.

_____ (2000). *Beyond Room 109: Developing Independent Study Projects.* Portsmouth, NH: Heinemann—Boynton/Cook.

_____ (March–April 2008). Team Notebooks: Writing to the Next Level: Part 1. *Soccer Journal. 52 (2),* 28, 30–31.

_____ (May–June 2008). Team Notebooks: Writing to the Next Level: Part 2. *Soccer Journal. 53 (3),* 28-29, 46.

_____ (July–August 2008). Team Notebooks: Writing to the Next Level: Part 3. *Soccer Journal. 53 (4)* 24, 26, 28.

Lightfoot, M. & Martin, N. (Eds.). (1988). *The Word for Teaching is Learning: Essays for James Britton.* Portsmouth, NH: Heinemann—Boynton/Cook.

Luff, C. (2011, April 20). *10k training: intermediate runner schedule run a pr in the 10k distance.* About.com Guide, Retrieved from http://running.about.com/od/racetraining/a/10Kintermediate.htm

MacArthur, C. A., & Karchmer-Klein, R. A. (2010). Web 2.0: new opportunities for writing. In G.A. Troia, R. K. Shankland, A. Heintz (Eds.), Putting Writing Research into Practice (pp. 45–69). New York, NY: Guilford.

Martin, N. (1983). *Mostly About Writing.* Portsmouth, NH: Heinemann—Boynton/Cook.

Murray, D. M. (2005). *Write to Learn.* Boston, MA: Thomson/Wadsworth.

Nash, M. and Loomis, S. (1998). *Pushing the Limits: A Nordic Skiing Saga.* Portsmouth, NH: Peter Randal Publishing.

National Commission on Writing in America's Schools and Colleges. (2003). *The Neglected R: The Need for a Writing Revolution.* New York: College Board.

Paley, V. (1981). *Wally's Stories.* Cambridge, MA: Harvard University.

Parker, R.P., and Goodkin, V. (1987). *The Consequences of Writing: Enhancing Learning in the Disciplines.* Upper Montclair, NJ: Boynton/Cook.

PBS Educational Resources: Theory of Multiple Intelligences. (n.d.). Retrieved from http://www.pbs.org/wnet/gperf/education/ed_mi_overview.html

Pruden, V. (1987). *A Conceptual Approach to Basketball.* Champaign, IL: Leisure Press.

'Serena's No Cheat,' says father. (2007, July 3). *Mail Online,* Retrieved from http://www.dailymail.co.uk/news/article-465858/Serenas-cheat-says-father.html

Smith, L. and Fershleiser, R., (Eds). (2008). *Not Quite What I was Planning: Six-Word Memoirs by Writers Famous and Obscure.* New York: Harper.

Strong, W.J. (2001). *Coaching Writing: The Power of Guided Practice.* Portsmouth, NH: Heinemann—Boynton/Cook.

Teaching Today: Helping English Language Learners in the Classroom. (n.d.). Retrieved from http://www.glencoe.com/sec/teachingtoday/subject/help_ELL.phtml

Wormser, B. and Cappella, D. (2004). *A Surge of Language: Teaching Poetry Day by Day*. Portsmouth, NH: Heinemann.

Zinsser, W. (1988). *Writing to Learn: How to Write—and Think—Clearly About Any Subject at All*. New York, NY: Harper & Row.

Index

A

Advice to Athletes/Writers 112
Ali, Muhammad. 138
American College of Sports Medicine 108
Athlete
  Notes 8, 13
  Writing 8, 13, 15, 20–21, 32–33, 37, 39, 41, 42–44, 46–47, 58–62, 64, 65, 66, 76, 86, 87, 92, 93–94, 106, 110, 114–115, 118, 119, 120,121, 125–127, 134–135, 150, 151, 174
Atwater, James. 107
Audience 107, 125, 163–164

B

Because Writing Matters 180
Bennett, Christian. 115
Bennett, Willy. 118
Blank Pages 22, 111
Blogs 1, 4, 26, 36, 106, 112, 125, 126, 127, 129, 130, 131, 143, 148, 160, 163, 164, 176, 177
Bloomfield, Charlie. 134–135
Britton, James. 107
Brown, Griffin. 93

C

Carey, Grant. 178
Capacity Analysis 41–43
Chadbourne, Adam. 115–116
Chamberlain, David. 147, 149–153, 155–156, 158–164
Coach
  Effective 3, 6, 15, 22, 39, 44, 117–118, 128, 134
  Learning 2–3
  Reading 2, 8, 13, 24, 36–39, 40–41, 48, 56, 57, 60, 169, 178
  Writing 175

Coach's Letter 131, 132
Coffin, Sam. 93
Comical Moments 67
Competition Analysis I 8, 10, 23, 24, 25, 55–72, 89, 169, 185
  Best/Most Comical Moments 67
  Found Poem 67
  Halftime or Post Game Talk to Opponents 66
  Note to Opponent 63, 65–66
  Note to Opponent's Coach 66
  Note to Team Member 67
  Photo Captions 68–69
  Synthesis 62–63
  Video Comments 67
Competition Analysis II 8, 25, 73–84
  Game Films 82
  Player of the Game 82
  Sportscaster Commentary 83
  Reenactments 83
  Word Clouds 84

D

Demand Analysis 41, 44
Double-Entry Journals 120

E

Edwards, Amy. 14, 15, 185
Engblom, Thor. 166, 167
English Language Learners (ELLs) 170–172, 181
End of Season Journal 93

F

Facebook 1, 26, 45, 127, 129, 130, 137, 166, 168, 176, 177
FAQs 165–182
Found Poem 67–68
Free Writes 113

G

Game Films
  Player of the Game 82–83
  Sportscaster Commentary 83
  Reenactments 83
  Word Clouds 84
Game Reports 174–176
Gauvin, Kyle. 119
Goestenkors, Gail. 105
Good Teammate 118
Goodwin, Ryan. 92
Grawrock, Matt. 8, 169
Guided Writing 114

H

Halftime or Post Game Talk to Opponents 66
Health Report 125–127
Homka, Jennifer. 174
hooks, bell. 25
Hostage, Meg. 106

I

Individual Education Plan (IEP) 172
Injury Rehabilitation 16, 19, 125–127

J

Journals 105–128, 173
  Activities 117–128
  Benefits 109, 154
  Choice 130
  Coach's Letter 131, 132
  Cover Page 130–131
  Digital Options 130

Entries 113–128, 158
Frequency 129
Privacy 130
Prompts 22, 116–117, 130, 131, 133–143
Purpose 129
Quotations 131, 144
Template 129–145
Themes 145, 157
Tips 111

K

Keller, Mike. 61, 166
Kellogg, Matt. 93
Kent, Ryan. 184–185

L

Learning Styles 25–27, 172
Letters to Incoming Athletes 92
Listening In 77, 79

M

Making Meaning 142–143, 152–153
Match Analysis 14
Match Ratings 174, 176
McKenna, Chris. 93
Michaud, Nick. 125–127
Modes of Writing 106–107
Moore, Nicole. 85, 179
Murray, Donald. 108, 113, 180
Murray, Jason. 112–113

N

National Writing Project 180
New Athlete Information Form 92
Note to an Opponent 63, 65–66
Note to Opponent's Coach 66
Note to Team Member 67

O

O'Dwyer, Danielle. 110

P

Packing List 149, 171
Paley, Grace. 108
Performance Feedback 109, 110
Personal Evaluation Checklist 16
Phillips, Pete. 41, 44–45
Photo
Captions 68–69
Poetry 123
Player of the Game 82–83
Player Profile Sheets 29–30
Players' Instructional Manual 16
Poetry 122–125
Portaportal 177
Position Poem 124
Postseason 8, 15, 85–94
Writing Prompt 88–89
What Helped You Learn 89–90
Quotations Synthesis 90
Reading-in-the-Round 90, 91
Senior Letters 90
Practice 15
Pre/post game 14, 16, 17, 20
Preseason 8, 14, 29, 31, 33, 35–39, 45–53
Professional Organizations 180

Q

Quality at Bat 16, 18
Quick Writes 113–114, 115
Quotable Quotes 22, 24

R

Reading-in-the-Round 90–91
Reenactments 83
Richmond, Gavin. 174–176

S

Season
  Setting the Tone 34
  Organization 35
  Using Technology 36
  Record Keeping 36
Senior Letters 90, 91
Six Word Sports Story 177
Snap Shot 115–116
Sports Poetry 125
Sportscaster Commentary 83
Stawinski, Sheila. 109
Stills, Andy. 15
Stein, Gertrude. 165
Stress 108, 111, 112, 126, 154
Swallow, Eric. 76
Synthesis 62–63
System of Play (SOP) 70, 72
Szeps, Jonathan. 114

T

Tag a Teammate 121–122
Team Development 70
Team Notebook 8, 16, 22–23, 71, 72, 74–75, 114, 168, 169
Team Report Card 16
Team Social Networking Website 127
Themes 145
Thinking Partner 128
Three-Sentence Poem 124
Training Log 149, 150, 151
Training Plan 149, 163
Twitter 1, 129, 168, 176, 177

V

Verville, Joshua. 31
Video Comments 67

W

Weil, Simone. 111
Williams, Serena. 106
Word Clouds 84
Writing to Learn 108

Z

Zinsser, William. 108, 180